Urban
Transportation for
the Environment

The authors would like to acknowledge the encouragement and help of George Tolley, and the aid of Jay Norco, Todd Petzel, Jim Cavallo and Jim Neil.

Urban Transportation for the Environment

Richard O. Zerbe
Kevin Croke

Ballinger Publishing Company ● Cambridge, Mass.
A Subsidiary of J.B. Lippincott Company

Ballinger Studies in Environment and the Urban Economy - under the general editorship of George S. Tolley.

Studies in Environment and the Urban Economy, a special Ballinger series under the general editorship of George S. Tolley of the University of Chicago, is published in the hope that it will be a vehicle for the meaningful synthesis of environmental research.

Other books in this series:

Residential Fuel Policy and the Environment - Alan Cohen, Argonne National Laboratories, Gideon Fishelson and John Gardner, University of Chicago.

International Standard Book Number: 0–88410–325–0

Library of Congress Catalog Card Number: 74–14645

Printed in the United States of America

Library of Congress Cataloging in Publication Data

Zerbe, Richard.
           Urban transportation and the environment.

           1. Urban transportation—Environmental aspects. 2. Air—Pollution. 3. Automobile exhaust gas. I. Croke, Kevin, joint author. II. Title.
TD195.T7Z47   388.4   74–14645
ISBN 0–88410–325–0

Contents

List of Tables

List of Figures

xi

Foreword

One of the chief areas of environmental concern has been transportation pollutants. The importance of transportation, the magnitude of the control costs and the intensified interest in transportation as a user of energy have greatly heightened interest in finding measures to meet environmental goals with as little cost as possible.

Analysis of environmental measures has been hindered by lack of coordination among disciplines. Interdisciplinary approaches are needed which give adequate attention both to physical science relationships and to economic behavior and the economic determinants of costs. The study presented here is an integrated engineering-economic investigation. An important contribution is the development of an interdisciplinary methodology for assessing the merits of different transportation measures.

The study is concerned with air pollution problems arising from motor vehicles. Conclusions are reached regarding a wide range of alternative possible federal controls, local controls and mass transportation policies to reduce automotive pollutants.

The underlying research is from a project entitled "Environmental Pollutants and the Urban Economy," funded under the National Science Foundation RANN Program. The grant was made jointly to the University of Chicago and Argonne National Laboratory.

G.S. Tolley

Kevin Croke

**Urban
Transportation for
the Environment**

Chapter One

Regulatory Issues and Framework

THE NATIONAL SETTING

The national commitment to clean up the air in our cities began in earnest in
the late 1960s with the development of an elaborate regulatory framework.
Not surprisingly the automobile has been a primary recipient of attention
from this large scale effort. After all, the automobile accounts for 60 percent
of the nation's pollutants by weight and these pollutants are emitted in densely
populated areas at ground level. Automobile operation caused approximately
60 percent of the emissions of carbon monoxide, over half the total emissions
of hydrocarbons and 30 percent to 40 percent of the nitrogen oxides emissions.

However, the automobile is so inextricably tied up with our way
of life, with the nature of urban sprawl, and with the culture itself that any
significant regulatory program cannot help but have substantial effects. It is
important, then, to understand the nature of the environmental regulatory
effort aimed at transportation and the issues relevant to policy making in this
area.

Just as automobile and mass transit patterns influence city forms,
so also do urban forms affect the pattern of resulting pollution. The most
densely populated cities with the most clearly developed downtown areas can
be expected to have the most concentrated vehicle emissions. Thus, in general,
the older, more densely developed eastern cities can be expected to have
somewhat greater concentrations of vehicle pollutants, followed by midwestern
cities and finally western cities. This pattern is borne out by Table 1-1. Carbon
monoxide, the best indicator of automobile activity, declines as one passes
from eastern to western cities. New York records the highest levels because of
its well-developed downtown and its high population density. The higher readings for Los Angeles reflect the great importance of the automobile and the
very high number of cars per capita there, but these high readings also particu-

Table 1-1.   Estimated Maximum Concentrations of
Carbon Monoxide, 1977

	CO parts per million
New York	32.2
Chicago	27.3
Denver	12.1
San Francisco	12.2
Los Angeles	27.5

larly reflect the frequent presence of inversion conditions which allow concentrations of pollutants to build up.

The major effort to control automobile pollution has been federal. It was assumed that state regulation was for the most part unfeasible, and states are in fact preempted from regulating emissions of new cars before sale at retail. The federal program has involved three major parts. First, new car emissions of carbon monoxide, hydrocarbons and nitrogen oxides were to be increasingly regulated, culminating in *emission standards,* set originally for 1975, which required 90 percent to 95 percent of these pollutants from automobiles to be controlled. These federal requirements have been applied uniformly across the nation.

Second, the federal program has also involved the establishment of *air quality standards* for the major automotive pollutants, based on observed health effects of human exposure to dosage levels of carbon monoxide, photochemical oxidents and nitrogen oxides. Two of these pollutants, carbon monoxide and nitrogen oxides, are directly emitted by automobiles, while photochemical exhausts are created in atmospheric reactions in which automotive hydrocarbons are a constituent. These standards were in terms of maximum concentration over a specified time period. For example, the carbon monoxide standards required that concentrations of no more than nine parts per million would be allowed per an eight hour period or 35 parts per million for one hour, where parts per million is a measure of concentration.

Finally, in order to assure that this emission reduction program would indeed guarantee the attainment of the air quality standards, particularly in major urban areas, states were ordered to submit *"implementation plans"* to the federal Environmental Protection Agency (EPA). The EPA would evaluate the impact of the federal emission reduction program on the projected air quality within each state. In the event that federal air quality standards were not met even with the 90 to 95 percent emission reduction program, the state was required to pass additional environmental control measures.

Initially it was thought that this federal program aimed at regulating the allowable emission rates of automobiles would be sufficient to control the undesirable environmental effects of automobile use and meet air quality goals.

More recently it has become apparent that state and local authorities may have to initiate measures, particularly in large urban areas, in addition to the federal program. The extent of the failure of the federal program to meet the air quality goals is strikingly indicated by Table 1-2, which shows a sampling of cities not expected to meet the air quality goals by 1977 with the federal program alone. Approximately 38 metropolitan regions throughout the country were reported to require some form of additional local emissions control. Even as late as 1985, 12 regions will fail to meet the standards without supplemental programs. Thus the present federal program will not achieve by itself the required air quality level. Moreover, some of the federal new car standards have been increasingly criticized, especially by industry, as being too costly.

This situation has created the need to look at the relationships between the state and federal efforts, to determine if the state and local roles should be enlarged and to seek the best combination of programs. Meeting this need is the central concern of this book.

As Tables 1-1 and 1-2 show, the areas with the most severe environmental problems associated with transportation are the larger cities, especially those which are densely populated, those with well-developed downtown sections and those with unfavorable climatic conditions. The methodology developed here could be applied to any of these cities. A detailed analysis of one reasonably typical city should yield greater insights than only the general consideration of the problems of several cities.

Chicago was chosen as an appropriate area. In Chicago, because of the intense development of traffic-generating activities in the central city, the diverse commercial-industrial base of the city, and the existence of a highly developed freeway and mass transit system, the evaluation of a full spectrum of local environmental transportation control measures is possible.

Table 1-2. Estimated Violations of Air Quality Standards, 1977

	CO	Oxidants
New York	x	x
Baltimore	x	x
Boston	x	x
Philadelphia	x	
Pittsburgh	x	
Dayton		x
Chicago	x	
St.Paul/Minneapolis	x	
Houston/Galveston		x
Denver	x	x
Salt Lake City	x	
Phoenix/Tucson	x	x
Seattle	x	
Spokane	x	
Los Angeles	x	x

URBAN TRANSPORTATION SYSTEMS

The problems of controlling pollution are inextricably related to the nature and development of transportation systems in urban areas in the last decades. An examination of this development is required to give a perspective with regard to air quality problems and policy.

Preceding World War II, both population and employment were concentrated within central cities and most travel occurred within development corridors that were well served by public transportation. Under this pattern of development transit lines serving densely populated areas were profitable and the carriers providing these services were generally under private ownership.

The post-World War II era has witnessed the growth of the suburban areas encircling the traditional central city. These population movements have led to significant changes in the urban structure which have contributed to the decline of public transportation carriers and rise in automobile use. Thus, the suburbanization of population during the past 20 years has aggravated the urban air quality problem.

Besides the suburbanization of the population, a later phenomenon has been the relocation of employment opportunities from the central city to the suburbs. This shift of employment opportunities—from the growth of manufacturing and commercial establishments—was due to the new population markets and labor pools in the suburbs, lower land costs, the availability of land for plant expansion and the increased use of highways to ship freight. This trend caused increased dependency on the automobile as the means of transportation for the work-trip and it resulted in increased dispersal of trips within the region. The private automobile, with its associated favorable characteristics including convenience, comfort and dependability, has been the dominant means of urban mobility in spite of its environmental consequences.

These population and employment shifts have been reflected in the Chicago area and have influenced the nature of its transportation system and mobile source air pollution problems. The Chicago transportation system is a mixture of public and private systems. Transportation demand is served by a system of six freeways which converge in the vicinity of the central business district and by both bus and rail commuter mass transit which converges on the central business area and carries a majority of its passengers to this area during the rush hour periods. As in most major metropolitan areas, there are two prominent traffic peak periods from about 7:00 to 10:00 A.M., and 4:00 to 7:00 P.M.

Public transportation was used for 23.2 percent of the work-trips in the region in 1970 and the automobile was used for 67.7 percent of the work-trips. By residential location, 36.2 percent of the residents of Chicago used public transportation, compared with 11.2 percent of the non-Chicago residents. Given the existing radial nature of the public transportation system, particularly in the suburban areas, it is difficult, if not impossible, for persons to make non-central business district [CBD]-oriented trips via transit. These non-CBD trips are being made by automobiles if they are made at all.

By far the greatest concentration of traffic and emissions occurs in the area of the central business district and, therefore, special note must be made regarding the traffic characteristics there. The Chicago CBD, an area of about 350 acres, contains the most intense commercial, retail and governmental concentration of activity within Chicago. Automobiles carry approximately 250,000 people into this area daily. An additional 350,000 people enter the CBD each day by means of the system of rapid transit and commuter trains. Figure 1-1, based upon the annual cordon count of the Chicago Department of Streets and Sanitation, indicates the relative importance of rapid transit and commuter rail systems as opposed to private autos, buses and taxis.

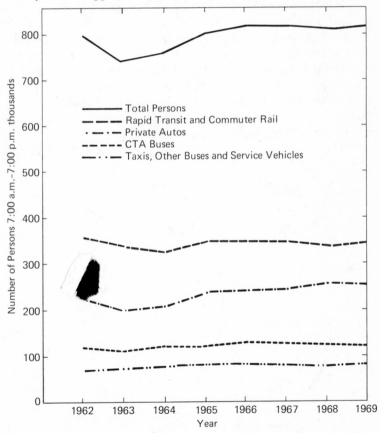

Figure 1-1. Number of Persons Entering the Chicago CBD by Various Transportation Modes.

Despite the fact that the Chicago transportation system as a whole experiences pronounced peaks in the morning and evening rush hours, an examination of the diurnal traffic patterns within the CBD would seem to indicate that, in terms of the vehicular miles generated, automobile traffic in this area is relatively constant from 9:00 A.M. to 5:00 P.M. Figure 1-2 indicates this pattern of traffic. Despite small peaks at about 8:30 A.M. and 4:30 P.M., it is clear that the total number of vehicles recorded operating in the CBD remains approximately constant throughout the day. It is during this period of uniformly high traffic activity that the highest carbon monoxide concentrations in the city were recorded.

URBAN AIR QUALITY

The transportation patterns of most major cities, including Chicago, have produced characteristic patterns of air pollutant concentrations. The highest recorded readings of automobile pollutants are normally found in central business districts with progressively lower pollutant concentrations as distance from the CBD increases. These air quality patterns have become the subject of extensive monitoring by federal and local agencies in major cities to determine the effects of the federal emission reduction programs. Such monitoring in Chicago is done routinely by the federal Environmental Protection Agency in downtown Chicago, and air quality measurements from this station are the basis of federal and state evaluations of the effectiveness of pollution abate-

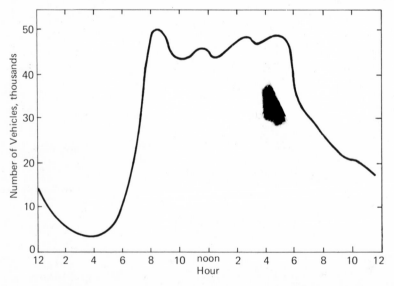

Figure 1-2. Typical Daily Vehicle Activity Within the Chicago CBD.

ment programs. Figure 1–3 shows a typical diurnal pattern of carbon monoxide readings. An examination of the figure shows that although peak periods of carbon monoxide concentrations do exist, the readings are consistently high throughout the day.

Analysis of the air quality data indicates that the major problem associated with transportation pollutants arises in the CBD and with respect to carbon monoxide (CO). The national primary ambient air quality standards for carbon monoxide are a maximum average of nine parts per million eight hour concentration and 35 parts per million maximum one hour concentration. Since the primary one hour standard of 35 ppm has not been exceeded in Chicago at any of the above locations, the basis for determining the required emission reductions is therefore the eight hour average.

The basis for determining the required carbon monoxide emission reduction in the region will be either the air quality data obtained during 1971 at the federal station or the 1973 data from this station: it is unclear at this point whether the 1971 or 1973 data will be used. On June 4, 1971 an eight hour concentration of 22.9 ppm was measured. This was the highest measurement in the base year of 1971. The second highest concentration measurement in the base year occurred on June 1, and again on June 4, when 18.9 ppm of CO was measured for an eight hour period. According to federal guidelines, the second highest reading is used as the basis of estimating the required emissions reductions. For Chicago the second highest reading is twice the standard

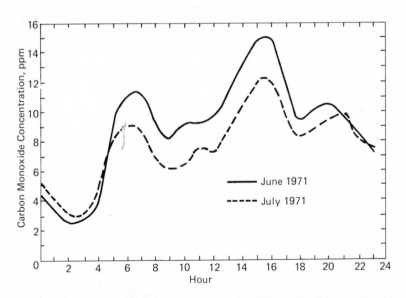

Figure 1–3. Diurnal Patterns of Carbon Monoxide Observations at the Chicago CAMP Station.

of nine ppm. Assuming air quality concentration to be directly proportional to emission rates, a reduction of about 50 percent in air quality concentration and, therefore, about a 50 percent reduction in emission rates is required in order to insure that air quality standards will not be exceeded.

OBJECTIVES AND STRUCTURE OF THIS STUDY

The purpose of this book is to develop a methodology for choosing a mix of policies that will attain environmental goals at least cost. The analysis is most immediately useful in searching for efficient ways to meet federally regulated air quality standards. More generally, the analysis can be used to find the least costly way of achieving air quality goals if the federal standards are taken as subject to change.

Three major policy approaches for controlling automobile emissions may be delineated. Within each of these approaches there is a variety of specific measures to be implemented. The first approach is federal regulation of automotive emissions. The second is local automotive controls, and the third, fostering travel by less polluting modes. A chapter is devoted to each of these approaches.

Chapter Two is concerned primarily with costs and effects of federal new car standards. Major questions have arisen regarding the timing of the federal program. There has been intense criticism of the timetable of the emission reduction program, especially by the automotive industry, which claims that control devices could not be engineered, mass produced and installed on a nationwide basis in accordance with the federal requirements. Questions have arisen as to the wisdom of requirements to meet the federal air quality standards prior to the time that the effects of the emission standards would be felt. The economic costs of the relationship between air quality and emission standards timetables need to be identified.

Another issue concerns the uniformity of the federal emission standards. Chapter Two examines whether this uniformity is necessary and whether there are gains to be had from introducing a more flexible program. In particular, Chapter Two considers the desirability of a two car standard for the nation based on a distinction between urban and rural areas.

Finally the question is raised whether alternative technologies will change the costs of reaching more stringent standards significantly enough to make waiting for the development of this technology worthwhile. If this is the case, what interim measures might be used to control automobile pollutants? A related issue concerns the adverse health effects of the technology currently being considered.

In order to investigate these issues, a series of technical models is developed in Chapter Two. A flexible and detailed emission model is provided which predicts emissions for a wide range of vehicle characteristics. This model is interlinked with models determining the characteristics of the vehicle population and the transportation network. The combination of these models with a model for determining the cost of the various policies allows the calculation of cost-effectiveness of the policies.

Chapter Three attempts to define feasible local transportation emission strategies and to evaluate these. The two general types of strategies considered are:

1. In-use Vehicle Emission Control Programs. These measures would include any additional emission reduction program which is aimed at reducing the emission rate of those model-year vehicles not subject to the most stringent new car standards. Such measures consist of programs to retrofit older fleet vehicles with additional emission control devices, development of emission inspection systems designed to reduce emissions by requiring maintenance of those vehicles which have emission rates above a certain standard, and efforts to convert certain types of vehicles, such as taxi or truck fleets, to alternative fuels which do not have high pollutant emission characteristics.
2. Traffic Control Strategies. These strategies are based upon the fact that the emission rates of some of the pollutants from automobiles are inversely proportional to the speed of operation of the vehicle. Therefore, any measures which increase the average speed of vehicle traffic in an area will reduce the overall emissions of pollutants. Strategies include introduction of more sophisticated traffic signal systems, the banning of parking along major arterials, restrictions on freight deliveries during periods of highest automobile congestion and staggered work hours.

Chapter Four continues the examination of local strategies with an examination of mass transit strategies. Considerable interest has been generated in the use of mass transit as an environmental tool. A variety of mass transit strategies are considered, including tolls or licenses for automobile operation based on their congestion and pollution costs, reductions in mass transit fares, parking taxes, and the greater use of exclusive bus lanes. The relationship of mass transit to urban form and the consequent effect on pollutants are also briefly considered.

The policy issues considered in Chapter Four require the application of a sequence of behavioral and cost models. A model for predicting type of travel mode on the basis of behavioral characteristics is presented and used to determine the modal split for the policies. This model is combined with a congestion model by which the congestion effects and congestion costs associated with each of the policies can be determined. An economic model of optimum highway use is presented to determine the appropriate congestion tolls. Finally, the costs of changes in mass transit ridership in response to various policies are calculated by a mass transit cost model.

Chapter Five traces the methodological and policy implications developed. It attempts to point to directions in program planning, methodology and policy which appear fruitful in the further development of an environmental regulatory framework for transportation.

For all the policies analyzed in this book, the main quantitative tool is the cost-effectiveness ratio which enables comparison of the costs and the effectiveness of each environmental control strategy. The approach is less general than a benefit-cost approach estimating the benefits and costs of each program. At this stage, usable estimates of benefits of reducing automotive pollution are not available. The cost-effectiveness approach ranks the policies in the same relative order as a benefit-cost analysis so that the order in which the policies would be recommended would be the same. As further information becomes available on benefits, the benefit-cost approach will allow estimation of the point at which the less attractive policies would not be considered.

Such quantitative analysis alone is rarely adequate by itself to generate policy choices. Thus, in the policy considerations here an attempt is made to account for social and political issues as well as the quantitative results. The recommendation that some particular policy be implemented is not nearly as important as ensuring that an adequate evaluative framework is provided. The most unique contribution of this book is to develop an integrated method combining behavioral and engineering models to meet this need.

Chapter Two

Federal Policy for Control of Transportation Emissions

Emissions from automobiles have been increasingly controlled since 1968 and especially since 1970. Under federal law these controls are scheduled to become more stringent for several years to come, with automobile emissions ultimately controlled until emissions are about 5 percent of their precontrolled levels. The increasing requirements visualized are as follows:

Auto Emission Reductions Below Precontrol Levels

Standards	HC	CO	NO_x
1970 Standards	53%	61%	0
1973 Standards	66%	67%	32%
1975 Federal Interim Standards	83%	83%	32%
Most Stringent Standards	95%	96%	93%

Very substantial reductions in automobile emissions are thus expected under the federal program. This program is aimed at reducing emission rates for new model automobiles both by the installation of pollution control devices and by readjustment of certain of the internal operating mechanisms of the vehicle.

The process by which emissions occur and are controlled has been well documented [4, 13] and will be only briefly described here. Basically, vehicles emit pollutants from four sources: the fuel tank, carburetor, crankcase and engine exhaust. Hydrocarbons are emitted from fuel tank and carburator due to vaporization losses from the fuel. Fuel vaporization takes place in the carburator after the car is turned off but while the engine temperature is still high. Vaporization in the fuel tank occurs when the fuel tank temperature increases. The emission of hydrocarbons from the crankcase occurs because a portion of the combustion gases leaks past the piston rings during the compression and power cycles, and escapes into the atmosphere. Both hydrocarbons and carbon monoxide are emitted from exhaust gases as products of the incomplete combustion of the fuel-air mixture. Nitrogen oxide is also emitted from the exhaust by reason of the association of nitrogen and oxygen in air under the condition of the high temperatures of combustion.

In order to reduce emissions to the requirements of the federal new car standards, several basic types of controls are possible. Three systems are presently in use: a crankcase ventilation system which draws the gases that leak past the piston rings into the combustion chamber instead of allowing them to vent directly into the atmosphere; an exhaust emission control system which oxidizes CO and HC in the exhaust system; and a series of adjustments in the vehicle's operating parameters which lower the amount of CO and HC produced in the cyclinders.

The federal new car program requires the installation of progressively more efficient control mechanisms to reduce emissions during the 1970s. The effectiveness of the new car standards program depends upon the reliability and effectiveness of these devices as they are introduced into increasing percentages of operating motor vehicles.

ESTIMATION OF FEDERAL PROGRAM EFFECTS

The Emission Factor Model

For air quality control planning purposes, reductions in emissions rates are reflected in changes in automotive emission factors.[17] Emission factors are average emission rates (normally given in grams per vehicle miles) which are derived from a standardized test procedure, such as the 1975 federal test procedure which attempts to simulate an average urban trip. In this procedure, autos are operated on a dynamometer which measures engine power over a scheduled cycle of speed changes, accelerations and decelerations while the total emissions are collected in a bag and their total mass determined. The emissions are divided by the total trip length; thus, a measure of grams per mile over the "urban driving cycle" is produced.

These emission factors describe the emission rates for each individual model-year vehicle. In order to account for increasing emissions with increased automobile use, a set of emission "deterioration factors" has been utilized which accounts for wear and tear of the vehicle, as well as vehicle pollution control device deterioration. Emission factors will of course be specific to a vehicle type—private car, fleet vehicle, light duty truck, diesel—since these vehicles have different operating characteristics and different emission control requirements based on federal standards.

An average emission factor $\overline{EF}_{T,k}$ for year T and vehicle class K can be expressed as follows:

$$\overline{EF}_{T,k} = \sum_{t=T-L}^{T} P_{t,k} \, EF_{t,k} \tag{2-1}$$

where $EF_{t,k}$ is the emission rate for vehicle class K and model year t—i.e., a vehicle $T-t$ years old. $P_{t,k}$ is the percentage of the total vehicle miles traveled by vehicles in class k which is attributable to vehicles $T-t$ years old. The weighted factor accounts for the fact that the emission resulting from a mile traveled by an average vehicle in class k will vary depending on the age of the vehicle so that emission rates must be averaged over the number of model year automobiles on the road in year T.

The $P_{t,k}$ are actually derived from two estimates. The first is the annual vehicular mileage per automobile for an automobile $T-t$ years old. The second factor relates to the number of automobiles on the road in year T that are $T-t$ years old. The multiplication of these factors yields the vehicle's miles attributable to a given model-year.

Adjustments in Emission Factors for
Speed and Operating Temperature

The emission factors calculated by Equation 2-1 were relevant to vehicles traveling at an average speed of 20 mph. In addition, it is assumed that the automobile must operate at the conditions evaluated by the average urban driving cycle test. This cycle assumes that the automobile starts the cycle with a "cold" engine and ends the cycle (roughly 7.5 miles) in "hot" operating mode. The emission rate determined by this method is the average of the rates determined during cold and hot operating modes.

The speed and operating temperature assumptions must be viewed critically, especially when calculating the emissions from automobiles traveling in a central business district. The average speeds in major business centers are nearer 10 mph than the assumed 20 mph. They may reach 40 mph or more, however, on freeways. The importance of this speed variation is that emissions of CO, HC and NO_x change with the average speeds of travel of automobiles. Several studies have shown that higher average vehicle speeds are associated with lower emission rates of CO and HC per vehicle mile. The situation with NO_x emissions is reversed, with higher speeds causing higher emission rates. In order to account for variations in emissions due to travel on freeways, arterials and collectors, speed-adjustment multipliers are used to alter the emission factor applicable to vehicular operation on different street classifications. The difference between freeway emission factors and arterial factors for CO, HC and NO_x is indicated in Figures 2-1 and 2-2 for the years 1971–1980. For HC and CO, higher speeds decrease the emission factor substantially by 40 percent and 60 percent. For NO_x, however, higher speeds can increase the emissions by 10 percent to 20 percent.

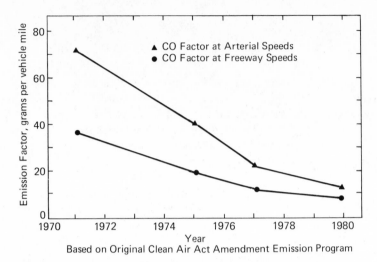

Figure 2-1. Speed Effects: The Difference Between Freeway and Arterial CO Emission Factors.

The second adjustment in emission factors applied to an urban area has to do with the emissions generated during the time when engines are cold. [12, 17] The emissions during the cold operating portion of an average urban trip become increasingly significant in later model cars and will be most significant in post–1975 model-year vehicles. This is primarily due to the characteristics of certain of the automotive pollution control devices which are not active until reaching a "light off" temperature. Figure 2–3 shows the relationship between the emission factor for CO and the minutes of operation of a vehicle from starting (a surrogate for engine temperature) for controlled and uncontrolled cars. For the first four minutes of operation the emission rate is much higher in both controlled and uncontrolled vehicles, but on a proportional basis the importance of the "cold start" emissions is much more significant for controlled vehicles. Thus, it becomes increasingly important in the evaluation of vehicle emission reduction strategies to consider where urban driving is likely to involve colder engines, particularly when dealing with a controlled vehicle population.

The cold start emission effect may have its most significant implications in central urban areas, especially those located in colder climates. Typically, most of the vehicles operating in urban areas in the morning hours have reached normal operating temperature by the time they enter the urban center. The cold start emissions for commuter trips to the CBD are distributed over the suburban areas surrounding the city. The concnetration of vehicles parked in the center city area cool during the daytime. They are then started over a

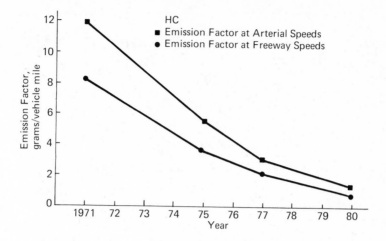

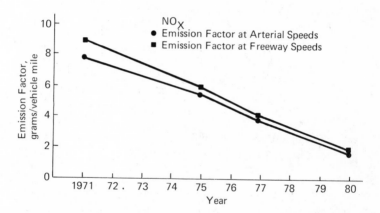

Figure 2-2. Speed Effects: The Difference Between Arterials and Freeways for HC and NO$_x$ Emission Factors Based on Original Clean Air Act Amendment Emission Program.

relatively short period of time during the evening rush hours. Since the emission rate of carbon monoxide for the controlled vehicle may be as great during these first few minutes as an uncontrolled vehicle, expected emissions for controlled vehicles in the CBD evening rush hour may be much higher than predicted if this phenomena is not taken into account.

The method of making this adjustment for cold start operations is to assign the fraction of the emissions from the vehicle during its first minutes of operation (provided the car has been idle for some hours) to the origin area

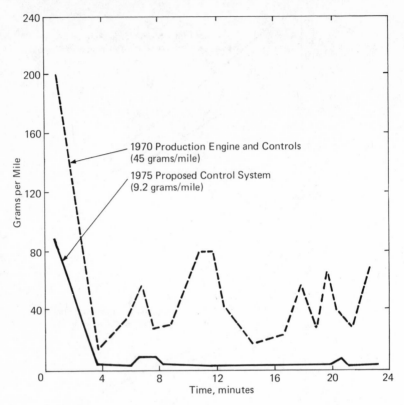

Figure 2-3. Typical Emission System Performance. 1972 Federal Test Procedure, Carbon Monoxide.

of the trip rather than averaging the initial high emission rate with the lower emission rate of the rest of the trip to calculate the average rate. Since the proportion of emissions during the first minutes changes depending on whether the car is controlled or uncontrolled, a new set of weights must be used for each model year to calculate the emission factor applicable to hot mode operations. Thus, Equation 2-1 becomes:

$$\overline{EF}_{T,k} = \sum_{t=T-L}^{T} P_{t,k} F_{t,k} E_{t,k} \tag{2-2}$$

where $F_{t,k}$ is the fraction of emissions generated during the time when the automobile was operating at higher temperatures in the urban driving cycle.

Fleet Vehicles

The age mix of vehicles in commercial districts differs from that in residential areas due to a greater percentage of taxi and fleet vehicle traffic. This difference alters the estimate of emissions. Taxis, for example, have an average total life of four years as opposed to over ten for regular automobiles. This fleet age effect tends to accelerate the reductions in emissions due to new car standards for fleet vehicles, and is particularly beneficial in the central city areas where fleet vehicles operate the most.

Table 2-1 shows emission factors which adjust for both cold start and fleet operations. The weighted emission factors for fleet vehicles are decidedly lower than for the private automobiles due to their newer age distribution. The private automobile emission factors shown here are divided into two parts: emissions associated with the hot operating mode and emissions associated with automobile startup. A weighted emission factor for the Chicago CBD is calculated by adjusting these vehicle class emissions factors by the percentage of vehicle miles traveled by each vehicle type in the area.

Shifts in Automobile Age Distributions

The emission factor is dependent on the estimation of vehicle mileage associated with different model-year automobiles. In this analysis the average vehicular mileage associated with a vehicle of a specified age was assumed to remain the same.[16] Thus, a two year old car in 1970 would drive the same number of vehicle miles as two year old cars in 1976. However, the estimation of the number of registered cars on the road of a given age in future years could not employ such a stationary distribution assumption. Basically, the increased costs of new lower polluting cars, both in terms of capital cost and operating costs, were hypothesized to cause a shift away from new cars during the first years that pollution control devices are introduced. This would tend to reduce the effectiveness of new car standards since the older higher polluting vehicles would be kept longer and used more intensively than they otherwise would have been.

This market shift effect necessitated the development of an automobile registration model to predict the age distribution of cars over time. Since the costs for pollution control offer no capturable return to the persons buying newer, lower emission autos, they are viewed as price increases with no corresponding quality change. Price series data for new cars were developed from pollution control cost data and the historical trend of new car prices. This price series was then combined with the price elasticity of -.9 (see appendix C) to arrive at a growth path of new car sales.

In order to estimate a shift in the age distribution of cars due to pollution control costs both new and used car registration must be projected. To project the retirement or scrappage of older model cars it was necessary first

Table 2-1.   Emission Factors Under the Federal Emission Reduction Program

	% VMT	1971	1972	1973	1974	1975	1976	1977	1978	1980
Carbon Monoxide (gm/mi)										
Private Cars Hot	.46	55.0	47.6	40.3	34.7	29.0	22.8	17.1	13.0	7.3
Private Cars Cold (gm/start)		106.5	96.7	86.2	77.4	67.1	57.9	48.8	44.0	36.8
Commercial and Government	.11	45.8	35.2	29.7	26.6	21.9	16.2	11.5	6.9	1.27
Rented and Leased	.07	39.7	24.7	21.1	21.1	15.4	3.9	1.1	1.3	1.26
Taxis	.21	45.1	36.2	29.2	26.8	21.7	13.2	6.8	3.8	1.97
Diesel Bus	.06	44.1	41.9	40.0	38.3	36.9	36.0	35.2	34.6	33.8
Heavy Duty Truck	.09	136.9	135.7	134.5	136.6	135.7	142.9	142.5	148.7	155.3
Weighted Emission Factor		57.6	49.8	43.9	40.6	35.8	30.33	25.59	23.09	20.03
Hydrocarbons (gm/mi)										
Private Cars Hot	.46	8.4	7.1	6.0	5.2	4.3	3.3	2.5	2.0	1.24
Private Cars Cold (gm/start)		8.6	7.7	6.8	6.3	5.3	4.4	3.5	3.1	2.35
Commercial and Government	.11	6.8	5.1	4.2	3.6	2.7	2.1	1.5	1.1	.51
Rented and Leased	.07	4.1	3.2	2.9	2.9	1.8	.7	.7	.5	.53
Taxis	.21	5.8	4.5	3.7	3.3	2.6	1.7	1.0	.8	.73
Diesel Bus	.06	8.0	7.2	6.5	5.9	5.4	5.0	4.8	4.5	4.25
Heavy Duty Truck	.09	22.0	21.4	20.5	19.5	18.4	17.9	17.1	16.8	16.4
Weighted Emission Factor		8.58	7.36	6.44	5.69	4.94	4.07	3.41	3.03	2.56
Nitrogen Oxides (gm/mi)										
Private Cars	.46	4.4	4.5	4.2	3.8	3.6	3.3	2.7	2.1	1.31
Commercial and Government	.11	4.8	4.8	4.3	3.6	3.2	2.7	1.8	1.3	.68
Rental and Leased	.07	4.9	4.6	3.0	2.6	2.7	2.5	.8	.5	.52
Taxis	.21	4.9	4.8	4.0	3.1	2.9	2.9	1.6	1.2	.8
Diesel Bus	.06	59.2	62.3	65.2	67.7	69.8	71.2	72.4	73.3	74.5
Heavy Duty Truck	.09	9.3	9.3	9.3	9.3	9.3	9.2	9.2	9.2	9.2
Weighted Emission Factor		8.31	8.51	8.20	7.88	7.84	7.71	7.01	6.63	6.18

to relate the increased prices of new cars to the prices of used cars. One expects that autonomous changes in new car prices due to pollution control costs will result in an increase in used car prices as there is a substitution away from new cars to used cars. In order to estimate a series of used car prices, equations of the following form were tested:

$$P_i = \alpha + B_1 P_{i-1\,(t)} + B_2 P_{i-1\,(t-)} + B_3 P_{(i-1)(t-2)} + \cdots \qquad (2\text{-}3)$$

where P_i is the price of an automobile of vintage i; P_{i-1}, vintage $i-1$; and t, a quarterly time subscript. Used car prices by quarter were estimated by a sample of prices in the *Detroit News*, 1957–1972, adjusted for depreciation. The results showed that price changes of one model-year affect primarily the next closest model-year. Using this model, it was possible to insert new car price predictions into the previous equations and to arrive at a matrix of projected used car prices.

It is hypothesized that three factors affect the retirement rate of vintage i autos: the projected used car price estimated by the previous equation, disposable income, and repair costs. Regression equations were developed to predict scrappage rates based on these factors. By applying the projected scrappage rate for used cars and the projected sales rate of new cars to the present vehicle age distribution, one obtains the shift in the age distribution of vehicles over time due to the federal program. The results of the application of this model are shown in Figure 2–4. Two age distributions are given, one for 1971 and a projected distribution for 1977.

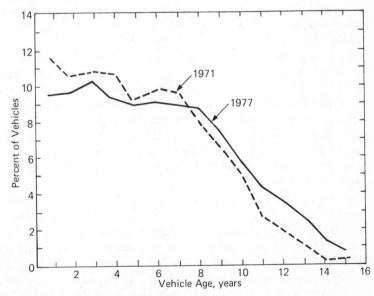

Figure 2-4. An Illustration of the Differences in Age Distribution Over Time.

The significance of using such models to predict vehicle age distributions lies not only in the fact that the emission control costs alter the automotive market but also in that for urban areas the market for cars is decidedly different than for the country as a whole. Urban areas have a tendency to have generally new model cars operating in them. Thus, urban air pollution should be reduced more rapidly because of new car standards. Emission factors using both national and Chicago metropolitan vehicular age distributions were estimated and it was found that factors using national age distributions were 20 percent to 30 percent higher for 1971 and 30 percent to 40 percent higher in 1975 than those based on the urban vehicular age distributions.

Estimating the Distribution of
Vehicle Miles

The emission factors for the Chicago region and for the CBD are applied to projections of traffic to obtain a pollution profile of the region. In order to estimate a geographical distribution of automotive hydrocarbons, carbon monoxide and nitrogen oxides, it is necessary to obtain vehicle mileage for different classes of vehicles on a geographically specified system. The Chicago Area Transportation Study, [CATS] the long range transportation planning group for the Chicago metropolitan area, has produced and calibrated a transportation model. The CATS planning model, similar to those used in many other major cities, is based on a standard traffic zone system and is used to simulate transportation activities in the eight county study area.

The procedures for projecting the future distribution and level of vehicular activity by this model have been reported by Creighton.[6] Figure 2-5 show a schematic diagram of this process. First, surveys are taken which determine the present distribution of trip making within the region and relate trip-generation intensity to the present pattern of land use. Then, a projection of the future land use intensity and configuration is made by distributing regional estimates of the total growth in population and employment in the region to subregional areas. This distribution in the Chicago model was determined on the basis of the availability of undeveloped land in subareas and the distance of subregional areas from the central business district. By applying present trip generation intensity factors to future land use, a distribution of future trip origins can be projected.

These trip origins by subregion must be linked to destinations. This is done using an "intervening opportunity" model. The basis of this model is that the probability of having a trip end in a given subregion is related to the number of opportunities for satisfying the purpose of the trip that lie between the origin of the trip and a potential subregional destination. The greater the number of opportunities for satisfying a trip at destinations closer to the origin, the less the probability that more distant locations will be a destination for that trip. This model is calibrated using present origin-destination data and applied to determine the future distribution of origin-destination activity.

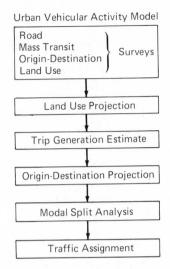

Urban Vehicular Activity Model

Figure 2-5. Transportation Component of Emission Model.

Once the origins and destinations of trips has been determined, a "modal split" model is used to estimate the number of trips involving private transportation. A traffic assignment model then allocates the automotive trips to alternative routes, based on a criteria of minimizing travel time. The total vehicle miles of travel in each zone are derived from the number of trips allocated in this manner. The trip travel time on each roadway type is calculated from a volume-speed relationship derived from empirical data.

The output of this model required for the air pollution emission model includes the distribution of trip origins, roadway vehicle miles on a zonal basis and vehicular speed. Pollutant emission calculation required an estimate of vehicular mileage for the years between 1971 and 1980. In order to estimate mileage on a zonal basis for these years a linear interpolation of the zonal mileage estimates for the years 1965 and 1980 was used. The interpolation scheme averages the vehicular mileage between 1965 and 1980 for each of the 1714 zones in the traffic projections.

Total Emissions
After the appropriate emission factors were calculated they were combined with the output of the transportation models to estimate pollutant emissions. The basic relationship used to calculate these emissions for each zone was:

$$E_{1,t} = VM_{1,a,T} \cdot \overline{EF}_{a,T} + VM_{1,f,T} \cdot \overline{EF}_{f,T} \qquad (2\text{-}4)$$

where:

$VM_{1,a,T}$ = vehicle miles traveled on arterials in year T in zone 1,

$VM_{1,f,T}$ = vehicle miles traveled on freeways in year T in zone 1,

$\overline{EF}_{a,T}$ = weighted emission factor for the year T adjusted to be appropriate to arterial speed operation, and

$\overline{EF}_{f,T}$ = weighted emission factor for year T adjusted to freeway speed operation.

The two sets of emission factors, arterial and freeway, are used to account for different average vehicular speeds and, therefore, the differing emission characteristics of arterial and freeway traffic.

As mentioned earlier, the emission model handles the calculation of cold start emissions by assigning a fraction of average trip emissions (depending on model-year) to the origin of the trip. The balance of the emissions (representing hot operation) is then distributed over the rest of the trip.

An emission calculation using speed-dependent emission factors with the local age distribution of vehicles within the Chicago area was used to generate emission maps for the Chicago region. An emission density map for CO is shown in Figure 2-6. The emission map indicates that the highest density of emissions occurs in the central business district of Chicago and along the major Chicago freeways. The reduction in these regional emissions for the six county SMSA over time is shown in Figures 2-7 through 2-9. These estimates are based on the original federal emission reduction program.

The emission reduction for just the Chicago CBD is calculated in a similar manner, but the emission factors and assumed vehicle miles traveled for different classes of vehicles are altered to account for the greater percentage of mileage due to fleet vehicles. Since the carbon monoxide standard for eight hours is the most critical in this area, calculations are shown for the reduction of CO emissions for 1971 to 1980 in Figure 2-10. Based upon the 1971 measured levels of CO in the CBD air quality monitoring station, the eight hour CO standards will be met if there is a 50 percent reduction in emissions from 1971 to 1975. According to the timetable of reductions, such a reduction will not occur until 1976. Further delays of the emission standards will, of course, produce additional delays in the attainment of this air quality level.

COSTS OF FEDERAL PROGRAMS

The procedures for estimation of the costs of new car standards involved estimating the costs associated with the installation and use of control devices.

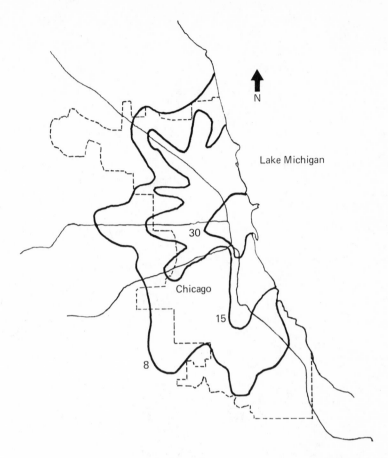

Figure 2-6. Isolines of Carbon Monoxide Emission Density (Initial Conditions, 1971) (ton per square mile per day).

Data concerning the costs of these devices as they apply to different model-year vehicles were collected from several sources.[3, 7, 8, 9, 10, 15] The total costs of the emission standards were considered in terms of capital, operating and maintenance costs. These may vary according to the model-year of the vehicle due to progressively more stringent standards, so that the automobile age distribution model was required to accurately calculate costs.

Total capital costs are found by multiplying the number of new cars by the unit capital costs in that year and converting to a present value. Thus for an eight year planning horizon:

$$\text{Capital Cost} = \sum_{i=1975}^{1983} Y_i K_i d_i \qquad (2\text{-}5)$$

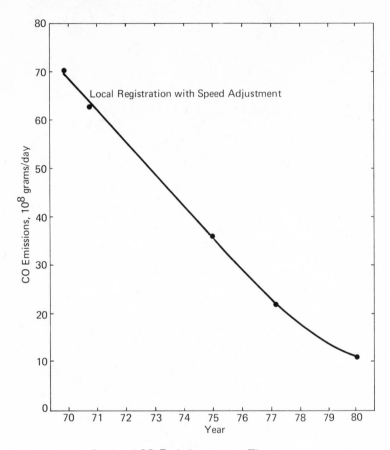

Figure 2-7. Regional CO Emissions versus Time.

where:

Y_i = number of new cars in year i,

K_i = capital cost for year i, and

d_i = discount factor.

Capital costs decline over time as the industry gains expertise in the mass production of pollution control devices. An examination of past data indicates that the capital cost in year i, K_i, is given by:

$$K_i = K_o - .31K_o \left(1 - e^{-0.337}\right) \tag{2-6}$$

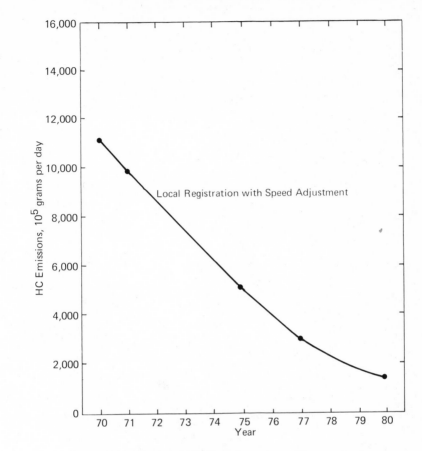

Figure 2-8. Regional HC Emissions versus Time.

Maintenance cost estimates are straightforward, consisting of the costs of maintaining the vehicle control systems, and expressed in terms of cost per mile. Maintenance costs are thus:

$$\text{Maintenance costs} = \sum_{1975}^{1980} Y_i^* M_i d_i \tag{2-7}$$

where M is the maintenance cost per vehicle mile and Y^* is vehicle miles.

It has been shown that the installation of control devices can reduce the mileage of automobiles substantially and thereby increase the operating cost of the vehicle. The cost of such a fuel penalty can be obtained from the following:

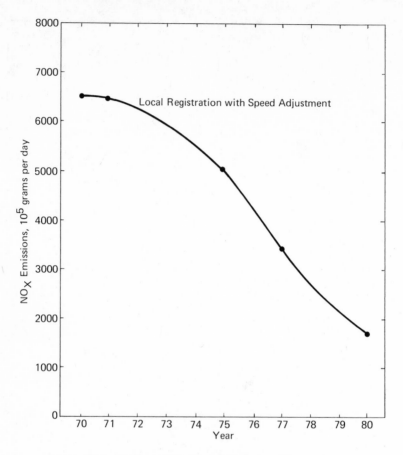

Figure 2-9. Regional NO$_x$ Emissions versus Time.

$$\text{Operating costs } (OC) = \sum_{i=1975}^{1980} + N_{ti} \left[\frac{AVM_t \cdot FP_t}{MG_t} \right] P_i \cdot d_i \qquad (2\text{-}8)$$

where:

OC = present value of the operating costs associated with the control device fuel penalty,

N_{ti} = number of registered cars of vintage t, in year i.

AVM_t = annual vehicular mileage assumed to be traveled by a vehicle in age group t.

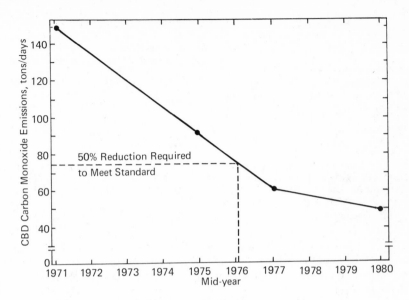

Figure 2-10. CBD CO Emissions versus Time.

MG_t = average mileage per gallon for this class of vehicles,

FP_t = fuel penalty expressed as a percentage for vehicles in age group t,

P_i = price of gasoline excluding taxes in year i.

d_i = discount factor in year i.

The expression in brackets represents the additional fuel per vehicle required because of the control system for a vehicle of age t.

The total and incremental costs of these programs are indicated below. Since the federal emission standards programs have been, and are, in a state of change, the significance of the cost figures and emission reductions presented in this chapter is derived more from the relationship between costs and emissions over time than from the exact cost or emission estimates for a given year.

EVALUATION OF THE FEDERAL PROGRAM

A number of characteristics of the above federal standards influence materially the costs and emissions associated with the standards. These characteristics include the pollutant regulated, the severity of the standards, their geographic coverage, timing of implementation and the methods used to define the standards. Each of these dimensions can be changed and thus can be considered as

Table 2-2.   Costs of Federal Standards for Chicago

	*Present value of eight year program base year 1973***	*Incremental Cost*
1970 Standard	297	297
1973 Standard	1101	804
1975 Intermim Standard*	1417	316
1975 Standard*	2333	916
1976 Standard [most stringent]	3953	1620

*The 1975 interim standards are those adopted when the 1975–1976 standards were de-layed. The 1975 and 1976 standards refer to the standards originally established under the Clean Air Act and scheduled for 1975 and 1976. At feasible gasoline prices the incremental costs of the 1975 interim standards are negative.

**Units given in millions.

a decision variable. Consideration of possible changes in these variables leads us to a discussion of the federal approach. In this light, several specific questions may be raised regarding the effects upon costs and emissions of altering these characteristics.

1. Are the most stringent federal automobile emission standards necessary?
2. Are the federal new car emission standards sufficiently inclusive to insure against important adverse health effects associated with the automobile?
3. Are improvements possible in the methods of defining the required air quality standards, the timing of these standards and the interaction of the timetables for air quality and emission standards?
4. Are there alternatives to the federal program which may produce more cost-effective results? In particular, is a multiple emission standard whereby emissions in urban areas are more stringently controlled desirable; are policies to control emissions of older cars more cost-effective than the most stringent new car standards; and finally, will alternative automotive control technologies become available in the near future which may be more attrac-tive than those now used?

Stringent Controls of New Cars

One of the most difficult questions in any pollution control program is centered on how much control is necessary. If the costs presented above are compared to present pollution reductions, it may be seen that the 1975 and 1976 standards show poor cost-effectiveness as compared with the other stan-dards. Interestingly, however, the 1976 standards are more cost-effective than those for 1975. The question arises, are these standards justified?

Existing knowledge puts total air pollution damage for the country as a whole at about $21 billion (see Appendix A). If we assume that all of this damage occurs in urban areas, how much is accounted for by automobiles? If existing indices for calculating the relative damage qualities of each pollutant are used to calculate the contribution of automobile pollutants to urban air damage, this figure is less than 20 percent. This estimate is considerably less than the contribution of automobile pollutants by weight, due in large part to the fact that carbon monoxide, the primary automobile pollutant, is less damaging per pound than many other pollutants.

Four billion dollars per year represents a generous estimate of damage from automobiles for the nation. Similar calculations for Chicago show that damages from automobile pollutants are between $125 and $186 million per year. The yearly cost of the 1975 and 1976 standards is about $400 million for the Chicago area. This damage by no means justifies the high cost of the 1975 and 1976 standards. The 1975 and 1976 standards will not add a great deal to pollution reduction in the next few years. In the next eight to ten years most of the pollution reductions occur because of the earlier standards and addition of more controlled cars to the automobile population. The implementation of these more stringent standards would mean that the reductions would be obtained about one year ahead of schedule. Moreover, since the effects of these standards would occur after 1975 they would be of no help in attaining the required 1975 air quality goals. In short, the evidence seems compelling that these more stringent standards are not, in fact, justified.

Whether or not the standards are justified in the 1980s, when automobile pollution may again start to increase, is a different question. As we shall see later, the probable or possible existence of new engine technology by that time may mean that these standards might be cost-effective. In the meantime, in terms of providing automobile manufacturers with economically correct incentives to develop alternative technologies, the government may be justified in taxing automobile manufacturers on the basis of uncontrolled pollution. This money could possibly be held in escrow as a performance bond. This approach, of course, is warranted only if it is decided that the approximately 95 percent level of control represented by the 1975 and 1976 standards is probably desirable for the 1980s.

The Secondary Health Effects of the Catalytic Muffler

The emissions standards for automobiles apply to HC, CO and NO_x. Automobiles, however, emit other pollutants. One pollutant of potential importance is lead. One advantage of the 1975 standards is that the associated control technology requires nonleaded gasoline and that therefore the emissions of lead will be less.

Not all of the secondary effects will, however, be positive. In order to meet the most stringent emission standards, new cars will be equipped with catalytic converters using platinum as a catalyst to reduce HC and CO emissions. These converters will emit platinum particles producing damages of unknown magnitude. That these damages might not be negligible is indicated by the fact that the Labor Department's threshold limit for potential toxicity is 100 times lower for platinum than for lead. Both present air quality and emission standards are silent on this issue.

The direct production of sulfuric acid by the converters is possibly of even greater concern.[5] Platinum acts as a catalyst in the presence of SO_x and oxygen, producing sulfuric acid in what is known as the contact process. The sulfur compounds produced by the automobile are a very small part of total sulfates produced, but it is very misleading to look at this figure. Automobiles with converters will produce sulfuric acid directly at ground level in areas of high population density. Research concerning the effects of this addition to the present sulfate burden indicates that adverse effects attributable just to this additional burden will be seen within two years after the introduction of the converters.

Deficiencies in Present Air Quality Standards

The criteria developed to determine if air quality standards have been met must also be viewed critically. A basic problem arises from the method by which the required emission reductions are estimated. This can be illustrated with reference to the Chicago situation. In 1971 the second highest reading of CO for eight hours (the measure used for estimating required reductions) was 18.1 ppm. Even though overall emissions declined in the city from 1971 to 1973, the second highest CO reading in 1973 was 19.3 ppm. According to federal procedures, this increased the required emission reduction from about 50 percent to about 60 percent.

Given the uncertainty of air quality measurement and the potential for localized air quality perturbations, the use of the second highest reading of CO to reflect the air quality condition of a city, or even the location in the city with the worst air quality, is hardly defensible. The use of other statistical measures indicates that air quality in Chicago, holding meterology constant, has improved rather than become worse over this period. This is sensible since CBD traffic has not increased and since emissions from cars have been increasingly controlled. Both the average CO concentrations and the average of those readings above the standard declined in this period. Evidently the distribution of readings above the standard is shifting downward, with both the average concentration and standard deviation of readings decreasing.

The inescapable conclusion is that air quality is improving and the emission reduction requirements should reflect this. The estimation of air quality, emission and environmental health effects is primarily a statistical procedure and, therefore, decisions based on a single observation must be viewed with suspicion.

Another deficiency in the definition of the standards arises because the use of standards implies that there are no adverse health effects so long as the standards are not exceeded. This implication is equivalent to assuming that damages are zero for changes in pollutants below the level of the standards. The use of standards in this way may produce policy decisions that are not always consistent with health goals. For example, since some strategies that reduce CO increase NO_x emissions, attempts to meet CO standards may increase NO_x emissions. These changes could be more harmful to health than the original levels of CO and NO_x.

Air quality standards are predicated on the basis of threshold health effects. Even if the standards concept is accurate, damages are unlikely to be zero for air quality levels below the standard. Moreover, there is increasing evidence that these effects are less a matter of thresholds and more a matter of continuous health responses.

ALTERNATIVES TO THE FEDERAL PROGRAM

An argument has been presented here that the more stringent new car emission standards may be undesirable at this time. Failure to carry through on these standards may, however, result in unacceptable levels of emissions in some locations for one or all of the three primary pollutants, HC, CO and NO_x. The failure to meet air quality standards raises the question of whether acceptable alternative control policies can be developed.

Retrofit of Metropolitan Area Vehicles
The installation of more stringent control systems on in-use vehicles represents one potential short-term alternative strategy for reduction of area-wide emission beyond that attained by the federal program. Given the possible delays in implementation of new car standards, such a "retrofitting" approach may become of great interest.

An analysis is performed here for the Chicago SMSA of the cost and effects of the 15 control devices now being marketed. (The description of these devices is given in Appendix E.) Calculations are made for the years 1975 through 1983 and shown in Table 2-3. In order to make these estimates, the age distribution of automobiles is projected using the registration analysis discussed earlier and the costs and effects of each device is thus determined. The effects of this program directed at in-use vehicles are those measured over and above the effect of the present federal standards.

In calculating the costs of each alternative retrofit program, the cost of many automobiles of different model-years must be computed over a period of several operating years. The costs of each retrofit device program consist of capital costs, operating costs and maintenance costs. The reductions due to each device are a function of the device specifications and the model-year car to which the control system is installed.

Table 2-3.   Cost-Effectiveness of Pollution Devices for In-Use Vehicles

	Reduction in SMSA emissions for 1975-1983 period (present value) (in 1000s of weighted tons per day)	Annualized cost of a ten year program (in 1000s)	Weighted Cost-Effectiveness
1. Speed Controlled Exhaust*	4,785	-100*	< 0.1
2. Spark-Retard	3,081	1,197	0.064
3. Positive Crankcase Ventilation	497	71	0.143
4. American Pollution Control System	6,503	1,038	0.160
5. Smog-Package Tuneup	343	57	0.166
6. Used Car Kit	1,623	366	0.277
7. Catalytic Reactor	19,223	6,851	0.356
8. Simple Exhaust Recycle	2,350	1,056	0.449
9. Dupont Flame Afterburner	24,845	11,633	0.468
10. Evaporation Control	940	502	0.534
11. Natural Gas Conversion	21,791	12,007	0.550
12. Air Bleed to Intake Manifold	1,973	1,126	0.571
13. Dual Catalytic Reactor	28,526	21,574	0.756
14. Ignition Timing with Lean Idle Adjustment	1,424	1,155	0.811
15. Alter Gas Conversion	261	266	1.020

*Costs are negative because of the improvement in gasoline mileage. Uncalculated costs associated with this device arise from interference with engine performance. While the true costs are certainly not negative they appear to be small.

As Table 2-3 shows, some very substantial emission reductions can be achieved with retrofit of in-use vehicles. Pollution reductions of approximately 40 percent or above are possible. This finding is consistent with other research in this area.[11] However, in order to produce effects of this magnitude, cost-effectiveness must usually be sacrificed. For policy purposes, a sensible criterion might be to consider those devices attractive with respect to their cost-effectiveness which also produce significant emission reduction effects. Three retrofit policies meet this criterion: speed controlled exhaust, the American Pollution Control System and the catalytic muffler. The speed controlled exhaust is especially attractive since it is the most cost-effective of all the devices and results in an eight percent decrease in automobile emissions for the 1975-1985 period. Reductions of about 11 percent are achieved with the American Pollution Control System, which is the fifth most cost-effective device. The catalytic muffler, while an effective retrofit device, is subject to criticisms already mentioned regarding its secondary health effects. Two other devices are almost as attractive as the first two: spark-retard and simple exhaust recycle. There would appear, then, to be about five devices worthy of consideration for retrofit.

The administrative and political feasibility of requiring large scale retrofitting of in-use automobiles must be considered. Older cars are usually owned by the lower income groups and therefore, to some extent, this policy puts an additional burden on them. In addition, older cars are more often found in nonurban areas where air quality standards are not endangered. Finally, the enforcement and administrative problems of monitoring the installation of devices on so many automobiles cannot be ignored. Such administrative costs for this type of program are likely to be substantial.

Multiple Emission Standards

Retrofit policies constitute a method of attaining equivalent reductions in pollutants without having to impose the most stringent new car emission standards. Another alternative to the present federal program would be to require stringent new car standards, but only for urban areas. This is accomplished through a system of multiple new car emission standards. Federal new car emission standards are presently uniform throughout the country; however, damages from transportation pollutants are heavily associated with urban areas so that uniform standards for all areas seem inappropriate. Not only are population densities much less outside of urban areas but, due to average speed conditions, the emission rates per car in rural areas are less than those for urban areas by about 50 percent for carbon monoxide and about 20 percent for hydrocarbon emissions. The question then may be raised whether a rural area should be required to have the same emission standards as an urban area. This issue gains added cogency from the fact that rural areas tend to be poorer than urban areas. Should rural Mississippi have the same standards as urban New York City?

Uniform standards involve a kind of vertical inequity as well as a geographical inequity. This type of inequity is best illustrated by example. Suppose that a locality has 100 equally rich and 100 equally poor inhabitants of similar tastes. Each of the rich inhabitants would be willing to spend $100 to eliminate pollution from his automobile if others were also required to eliminate their automobile pollution. Each poor inhabitant would be willing to spend $10. A device exists by means of which automobile pollution can be eliminated, and it costs $40. Each person in the community is required to pay the $40. The cost-benefit calculation shows clearly that the device should be adopted since the net benefit to the community is $3,000. However, the net benefit to the rich is $60 per person, or $6,000, while the net benefit to the poor is $10 per person, minus the $40 cost per person, or a negative $3,000. That is, the $3,000 net social benefit is attained because the rich gain a net benefit of $6,000, while the poor have a net loss of $3,000. Clearly, equity conditions are violated in that unequals (rich and poor) are treated equally and in that the redistribution of income is from the poor to the rich. The greater the number of different classes of people subject to uniform automobile emission regulations, the greater the inequity produced.

Thus, it seems likely that present uniform standards impose both efficiency and equity losses. However, given a recent argument that federal standards and regulations tend to be unduly uniform for bureaucratic reasons, the uniformity of present standards is not surprising. Indeed, the original arguments for federal pre-emption for setting emission standards may be incorrect.[18] In any event, an examination of possible gains from a multiple emission standard system are in order.

Three alternative geographic divisions to which the multiple emission standards could apply seem to warrant attention. These are: (1) division along urban-rural lines, (2) division on a state basis, and (3) division on a regional basis. Division along urban-rural lines would probably be the most efficient, neglecting administrative costs, because it would most closely reflect the air quality pattern of the country. Division along regional lines would probably minimize administrative costs, since fewer administrative units would be involved. A system set up along state lines would represent a compromise situation. Calculations are given here for a division only along urban-rural lines, specifically along lines of existing Standard Metropolitan Statistical Areas (SMSAs). The use of SMSAs provides an overly generous estimate for areas with air quality problems and would require that about 64 percent of the nation's cars meet the higher standard. Calculations are provided for the nation, for Illinois and for the Chicago SMSA. This SMSA distinction is chosen on the grounds that this division would provide virtually the same air quality for urban areas as the uniform standards, and for enforcement along the lines of existing political jurisdictions. Division along state lines, however, also seems quite feasible.

The procedure used in determining the cost savings from a two car standard was (1) to estimate the vehicle population of SMSA and non-SMSA areas, (2) to calculate the cost figures for a two car standard, (3) to compare these cost figures with those for a uniform standard, and (4) to estimate the increase in SMSA emissions. Both the national vehicle population and the Chicago SMSA vehicle population were estimated using the registration analysis presented earlier. National data and data for five important states indicate no difference in cars per capita between SMSAs and non-SMSAs. The correlation between population and automobiles is extremely high and thus the relative proportion of the number of cars in SMSA and non-SMSA counties is made on the basis of population projections for these areas. Vehicle age distribution, however, is considerably older in non-SMSAs, and it is assumed that the present age distribution for non-SMSAs is stationary over time.

The results of this analysis are striking and interesting. The cost savings from each two car strategy is substantial, as may be seen in Table 2-4. The savings based upon the distinction between different pollution damages in urban and rural areas thus cannot be ignored. These findings regarding the advantages of multiple as opposed to uniform standards apply regardless of the standards being chosen. With less severe standards, such as the 1973 standards, savings based on a two car distinction are still significant.

The objections which may be raised to the two car standard are those relating to enforcement difficulties and the problems associated with lower standards for cars operating in urban areas. This enforcement problem, however, seems tractable. For a system based along SMSA lines cars registered in SMSA counties might be required to bear titles or other certificates indicating that they meet the SMSA standard. Since an SMSA distinction would be on

Table 2-4. Savings From Two Car Standards Based on SMSA-Non-SMSA Distinction

	Present value of savings— eight year program at six percent (millions)	*Annual savings as compared with uniform 1975– 1976 standards*
1. Most stringent standards for SMSAs and 1975 interim standards for non-SMSAs	1059	171
2. Most stringent standards for SMSAs and 1970 standard for non-SMSAs	1524	245
3. Most stringent standards for SMSAs and 1973 standard for non-SMSAs	1188	191
4. 1975 Interim standard for SMSAs and 1970 standard for non-SMSA	4130	665

the basis of counties, enforcement would involve a distinction between registration in SMSA and non-SMSA counties. The division along state lines would perhaps be easier to enforce. The situation in California, where standards are different from the rest of the nation's, indicates that the enforcement problem can be handled.

The second possible problem of two car standards regards the possibility that the higher polluting cars may actually be used in urban areas. An attempt was made to investigate city center driving habits to determine if automobiles from outside the SMSA actually contribute significantly to vehicle miles in the Chicago CBD. To do this, a parking survey was conducted in downtown Chicago. It was found that considerably less than three percent of the automobiles came from outside the SMSA. In terms of vehicle miles traveled the percentage would be considerably less than this. Thus, in this case and probably in general the contribution of non-SMSA cars to the problem areas of urban cities is negligible.

Since rural areas have a disproportionate number of older cars, there already exists a form of two car emission standard. The market has already produced two classes of cars: an urban car, generally newer with a lower emission (not accounting for speed of operation effects), and an older rural car with fewer controls. The two car standard would reinforce this distinction by defining a regulatory mechanism to supplement the existing economic trend toward a distinction between urban and rural vehicular characteristics.

New Engine Technology

In the long run, we suspect that automobile and truck emissions are a question of engine design. Thus, the best alternative to the present procedures for controlling emissions may well lie with new technology. This section considers automotive parameter changes that are not directly related to emission control devices but which nevertheless affect emissions.

Some of the significant parameters to be considered are (1) compression ratios, (2) vehicle weight, (3) engine size and (4) engine type. The relationship between emissions and compression ratios is most important. Raising compression ratios while holding other parameters constant increases peak compression temperatures, lowers emissions of HC and CO, but raises the production of nitrogen oxides (NO_x). This decrease in HC, however, is offset by the increases in the reactive hydrocarbon emissions associated with the higher octane fuel necessary to achieve higher compression ratios. This will be especially true for newer cars which are equipped only for nonleaded gasoline and therefore cannot use leaded gasoline to increase the octane rating.

If vehicle weight is increased while engine power and compression are held constant, emissions increase: the engine will require heavier use of the power jets in the carburetor which increases emissions of HC and CO. The evidence is that HC will increase about as much as fuel consumption. Recent evidence indicates that CO emissions would increase by 30 percent of the increase in fuel consumption. Nitrogen oxides will also increase, since the harder-working engine will raise peak combustion temperatures. HC emissions will increase in vehicle weight for a constant horsepower engine. CO emissions would increase by 10 percent for a 120 percent increase in vehicle weight for a constant horsepower.

Although gas consumption increases with increases in engine size, larger engines do not necessarily produce more emissions. Indeed, a correlation of engine displacement and emissions gives a correlation coefficient of only .027, indicating that there is no statistically significant correlation between variables.[8] There appear to be three reasons for this:

1. The larger engine does not need to work as hard to get through a particular driving cycle. A larger engine can be tuned to minimize emissions because it has spare power, while a smaller engine may be tuned for maximum power in order to give adequate performance.
2. Larger engines with larger displacements have smaller surface-to-volume ratios and this tends to make engines cleaner.
3. Finally, there is a suggestion that emission control technology may be more efficient the larger the engine size.

It is possible, however, that this lack of correlation between engine size and emissions arises from the EPA test procedure for emissions. This test procedure consists of a driving cycle containing a series of idle, acceleration, cruise and deceleration modes. This means that larger engine cars will operate at lower throttle than cars with smaller engines. If cars with larger engines operate at the same throttle level as smaller engine cars, they may produce as much or more emissions as smaller engine cars.

For longer run periods substantial engine modifications are the best approach to emission reduction. It is apparent that this approach could yield substantial results by considering differences among current engines. Approximate calculations of the effects of using the less polluting engines are easily made. Average pre–1968 cars produced about 80 grams per mile of CO. However, certain American cars performed much better. For example, the 1971 American-made Avanti 350 cubic inch engine produced only about 6.5 grams per mile. In 1970 about 21×10^6 miles were traveled by automobiles on Chicago expressways. Pre-1968 cars then produced about 168×10^7 grams of CO. If only the Avanti 350 engines were used, 136×10^6 grams would have been produced. Emissions of CO with the less polluting engine would therefore be only 8.1 percent of what would be generated by an equivalent fleet of pre-1968 cars. Only nine percent of the HC emissions of the 1968 uncontrolled cars would have been produced. Similarly, the 1971 500 cubic inch Cadillac engine produces HC emissions which are only about 7.5 percent of those produced by the average 1968 car and which again are lower than the limit required by most of the emission standards.

The best hope of emission reductions may lie in more fundamental engine or fuel changes than are represented by the examples above. A wide variety of possible engine types and fuels exist. The more promising are the Wankel engine with thermal reactors, the "stratified charge" engine, the electronic fuel injection with emission control feedback, steam engines using water or, more likely, freon or organic working fluid, a wide variety of different gas turbine concepts, the Stirling engine and those using a gaseous fuel such as propane. We do not investigate in detail this wide variety of engines and fuel types, although some of these engines or fuels do represent real and viable alternatives.

Ayres reports the results of a substantial study undertaken to provide an assessment of the socio-economic impact of conversion to new low polluting engines.[2] Varieties of two alternative engines were considered: (1) a hypothetical regenerative free turbine and (2) several alternative designs of a hypothetical Rankin cycle engine. A basic conclusion of the study is that an overall ten year (six year planning and four year production) conversion period would be optimal. The ten year period is probably sufficient for conversion to the Wankel engine and more than sufficient for conversion to the stratified charge engine since this engine requires relatively little modification of existing engines. Other basic results of the study were that in terms of cost three of the 12 varieties of engines emerged as clearly superior, and that the two alternatives to the existing engine compared well with the conventional engine. The three most cost-effective engines were (1) the presently used Otto cycle engine with exhaust gas recirculator and dual catalytic converters; (2) a conventional regenerative gas turbine with ceramic burner parts; and (3) a Rankin cycle engine with conventional cylindrical burner-boiler design.

Although production costs are higher for the alternative engines, especially for the turbine, this is more than made up in savings in fuel costs and to a lesser extent in repair and maintenance costs. This savings in fuel costs is in fact likely to be considerably greater than earlier estimates and is expected to increase even further. Ayres used 23 cents as the price per gallon net of 11 cents taxes for leaded gasoline of 97 octane. Present value costs for a ten year program for the three engines using these low estimates of fuel costs are shown in Table 2-5.

Modification of the figures to account for higher fuel prices will increase the costs of the conventional car meeting the 1977 standards and lower the costs of the turbine. An additional point arising from the fact that the bulk of the savings from the alternative engines comes from fuel savings means that the benefits will be felt mainly by the lower income groups since this group mainly buys used cars. The bulk of an automobile's depreciation comes in the first years of its life. This means that the increased production cost of the alternative engines will be borne by purchasers of newer cars. Lower income buyers

Table 2-5. Costs of Alternative Engines

	1970 Conventional Car	*1970 Conventional Car With Emissions Controls to Meet 1976 Federal Standards*	*Gas Turbine*	*Rankin Cycle*
Costs for Years 1–3	3771.4	4212.9	3954.1	3785.8
Costs for Years 4–6	2418.3	2804.0	2597.7	2405.0
Costs for Years 7–10	1879.5	2178.9	1966.2	1832.1
Total Costs for 10 Year Program	8069.2	9195.8	8518.0	8022.9

purchase older cars so that they are little affected by the higher initial car price but they obtain the benefits of the lower fuel costs.

The present federal program has made a substantial, although not irreversible, commitment to a program of implementation aimed at meeting certain performance standards both in terms of air quality and automotive emissions. Much of this program may be praiseworthy, but serious problems remain. The high costs and unattractive cost-effectiveness of the most stringent automobile emission standards seem not to have received sufficient weight in the decision-making process. This is especially true in view of the alternatives available. However, these alternatives to the federal program require a greater flexibility in the federal program than it has hitherto shown itself capable.

The lesson here is that before the federal government makes a substantial commitment to a new program considerable efforts must be devoted to the planning stages of the program. In the same vein, greater flexibility should be devoted to deficiencies that become apparent in the course of program development. This flexibility is needed to improve the implementation planning procedures that determine the required emission reductions.

Chapter Three

Emission Reduction Strategies

The high cost of the federal program and the difficulty of obtaining required air quality with federal new car standards argues for a careful examination of alternative local emission reduction measures. The basic rationale for studying such measures is that violations of air quality standards in urban areas are related more to traffic characteristics in a specific location than to traffic conditions in the entire region. The local areas of greatest concern are the central business districts of major cities. It may be impossible or highly uneconomical to correct local air pollution problems in CBDs by the use of uniform or even multiple new car emission standards. Since these central areas have different traffic patterns, mixes of operating vehicles, and commercial and industrial transportation demands, their response to environmental policies will be significantly different than that of a region as a whole.

In order to evaluate the costs and effectiveness of local control policies, techniques are needed which will account for local conditions. This chapter will describe a series of such techniques, which will be applied in the Chicago area central business district. Four general types of local controls are evaluated and may be distinguished based on the mechanism by which they reduce emission. (The use of mass transit as an environmental tool may also be considered a local alternative, but consideration of this is delayed until the following chapter.)

1. Inspection-Maintenance Programs. The emissions per vehicle mile from an automobile are affected by its level of maintenance. Even automobiles that have been recently tuned may emit more than necessary if they are adjusted to obtain top engine performance instead of to minimize emissions. An inspection-maintenance system is a mandatory inspection system for all automobiles in a given area to assure that these cars are adjusted to the lowest emission operating parameters practical. Failure of an automobile to pass a

standard emission test requires that it be adjusted until the automotive emission rate falls below the standard. The thrust of such a program is to assure that those vehicles operating in the area are being maintained in a manner which will minimize the emission of automotive pollutants.

2.   Traffic Flow Strategies. It was pointed out in Chapter Two that the average speed of operation of an automobile is inversely related to its emission rate of CO and HC, but is directly proportional to the emission of NO_x. For areas of high congestion, special localized traffic controls may be effective in speeding up traffic and thereby reducing CO and HC emissions. Such measures include the introduction of computer-controlled traffic signals and the banning of parking along the sides of streets.

3.   Retrofit and Conversion Strategies. Local governmental agencies may wish to promulgate additional emissions control standards above and beyond the federal new car standards. These standards are normally aimed at fleet-operated vehicles and require the installation of control devices on in-use cars and trucks or the conversion of such vehicles to fuels that have low emission characteristics.

4.   Rescheduling of Traffic to Nonpeak Hours. Since violations of air quality standards normally occur during commercial weekdays, one way to reduce emissions during these periods would be to reschedule activities requiring automotive or truck traffic to off-peak or nighttime hours. Two such measures considered here are the rescheduling of deliveries to the central business district by trucks and the rescheduling of the working hours of commercial activities in the CBD.

These local strategies must be considered in conjunction with federal new car standards. The federal program will have its primary effects in reducing the emission contributions from private and fleet automobiles. This reduction will increase the relative significance of truck and bus emissions in the CBD. Using the models described in Chapter Two and accounting for the relative vehicular mileage of different classes of vehicles in the CBD, a table of the relative emission contributions for the Chicago CBD over time was developed (Table 3-1). As indicated, the new car standards decrease the private and fleet percentage contributions significantly, while the truck and bus percentage contributions rise to account for nearly half of the emissions of CO and HC and nearly three-quarters of the NO_x emissions. Another significant factor in evaluating the potential cost-effectiveness of local controls arises from the importance of fleet automobiles. Although these are only a fraction of the automobiles operating in the CBD, they account for approximately 40 percent of the emissions of private vehicles in 1975 because of their concentrated use in this area. These large contributions of emissions by trucks, busses and fleet vehicles in the CBD relative to the small number of such vehicles accounts for many of the findings of this study regarding the effectiveness of local control measures.

Table 3-1. Emission Contributions by Vehicle Category (values in percent)

	CO			HC			NO_x		
	1971	*1975*	*1977*	*1971*	*1975*	*1977*	*1971*	*1975*	*1977*
Passenger Cars	54.2	49.5	43.5	58.3	48.3	42.8	24.3	21.1	17.7
Commercial and Government	7.1	5.4	4.0	7.7	5.2	4.1	6.4	4.5	2.8
Rented and Leased	3.9	2.4	0.2	2.9	2.2	1.2	4.1	2.4	0.8
Taxis	13.3	10.2	4.5	12.5	9.5	5.3	12.4	7.8	4.8
Diesel Buses	3.7	5.0	6.7	4.9	5.7	7.2	42.7	53.4	62.0
Heavy Duty Trucks	17.4	27.3	40.6	20.4	28.7	38.9	10.1	10.7	11.8

The emission estimates derived in this chapter will be described in terms of percentage reductions of emissions in the CBD after the effects of the new car standards have been accounted for. Similarly, the costs of alternative local policies will exclude the cost of new car standards by vehicles operating in the CBD.

INSPECTION-MAINTENANCE

The purpose of inspection-maintenance systems is to reduce emissions by the testing of all or a portion of the vehicle population to ascertain whether they emit above a given emission standard. A certain percentage of vehicles will fail depending on the standard and the testing procedures. Failed vehicles then require subsequent tuneups or adjustments and retesting.

Testing Regime

Choice of a testing mode is the most important decision in instituting an inspection-maintenance system. A choice must be made among several types of testing regimes. The ideal testing regime is one that is quick, effective and inexpensive. Both effectiveness and costs will vary with the testing regime. Table 3-2 indicates the major tests now considered. For reasons of cost most jurisdictions including Chicago have adopted an Idle Mode test. Consequently, calculations here assume an Idle Mode regime.

The effectiveness of any system depends critically on the number

Table 3-2.   Testing Regimes for Inspection-Maintenance

Test Category	Description
Diagnostic: simple	This test involves setting engine parameters to some standard specifications. In particular, idle rpm, ignition time and the air-fuel ratio are adjusted to reduce emissions.
Diagnostic: complex	A loaded test* using sophisticated equipment to measure both exhaust emissions and performance of specific engine components.
Idle Mode	An unloaded test in which exhaust emission measurement is taken only while engine is not accelerating or decelerating.
Key Mode	This technique was developed by determining the minimum number and variety of operating modes required to expose emission problems. The 'key' modes are idle, low cruise and high cruise.
Transient Mode	A loaded test in which exhaust emission measurement is taken during idle, acceleration, deceleration and various cruise speeds. The 7 mode-7 cycle test formerly used by EPA is typical.

*A loaded test is one in which the engine is forced to simulate the stress of moving the weight of the car.

of cars which are inspected and on the percentage of emission reductions which can be anticipated. Several studies indicate an average reduction of approximately 33 percent for carbon monoxide and 40 percent for hydrocarbons under an Idle Mode regime; slightly increased emissions of NO_x can be expected from inspection systems.[8, 9, 27] Thus, when a car which is examined fails the test and is adjusted in order to pass, it is assumed to emit 67 percent of the CO and 60 percent of the HC per vehicle mile it previously emitted.

The Idle Mode inspection system is evaluated here for vehicles registered in four progressively broader geographic areas: (1) the city of Chicago, (2) Cook County (including Chicago), (3) the three most populous counties in the Chicago regions and, (4) the entire Chicago SMSA.

Emission Reduction Calculations

The following equation was used to relate the appropriate weighted emission factor for classes of automobiles and trucks after the inspection with the weighted emission factors calculated in Chapter Two.

$$\overline{E}_k = E_k [(1 - P) + P(1 - F) + PFR] \tag{3-1}$$

where:

$\overline{E}_k$ = weighted emission factor for either CO or HC assuming the existence of the inspection requirement in a given area,

E_k = weighted emission factor for vehicle class k calculated in Chapter Two (Equation 2-1),

P = percentage of vehicles operating in the CBD which are subject to the vehicle test requirements,

F = percentage of vehicles which fail the test and require adjustment (this is referred to as the rejection rate of the system), and

R = percentage reduction of pollutant emission due to a tuneup.

Thus, the vehicle population is divided into three categories: (1) those vehicles operating in the CBD but not registered in the study area and thus not affected by inspections $(1 - P)$; (2) those which are registered in the area, operate in the CBD and pass the inspection $P(1 - F)$; and (3) those which have the inspection and fail (PF). This last class must have a tuneup which reduces emissions of CO by 30 percent and HC by 40 percent, which accounts for the lower emission factor of Equation 3-1. The new weighted emissions factors are multiplied by the appropriate vehicle miles in the CBD.

Calculations were made for a variety of rejection rates (F). The most cost-effective rejection rates have been found to be between 10 percent and 30 percent.[10] Higher rejection rates require maintenance of cars capable of progressively less improvement. The calculations reported here assume a composite rate of 30 percent, since this is approximately the value administrators in Chicago expect for private automobiles. This rate is the estimate of the weighted average of the rejection rates for various model-year cars. Idle Mode testing by the Chicago Lung Association and Atlantic Richfield Company substantiates an overall rejection of approximately 30 percent. For commercial vehicles a 45 percent rejection rate was employed. The higher rate was used because of the greater average vehicular mileage and deterioration of fleet vehicles which leads to higher emission rates. For similar reasons, taxis and rented vehicles have a still higher rejection rate of 70 percent. Thus, in areas of higher commercial automotive use the effect of the inspection-maintenance system is greater.

In order to apply the emission factor (Equation 3-1) it is necessary to know the vehicle miles by vehicle class generated in the CBD, since the rejection rate for fleet and commercial vehicles is higher than for private automobiles. It is also necessary to know the origin of vehicles operating in the CBD, since those vehicles registered outside the inspection jurisdiction but driven into the CBD will be unaffected by the inspection testing program.

A survey of the CBD indicated a vehicle mileage proportion of 54 percent due to private cars and 46 percent due to commercial and fleet operations. In order to determine the origin of cars operating in the CBD a parking lot survey was taken in the area.[2] The results of this survey compared closely with other earlier surveys [11, 21] and indicated that approximately 40 percent of the private cars operating in the CBD came from outside Chicago.

Based on the foregoing data, overall emission reductions of 5.5 percent for CO and 6.2 percent for HC are computed for the CBD based on the Chicago inspection-maintenance system. Nitrogen oxide emissions are slightly increased by inspection-maintenance. As control devices for these emissions continue to be installed, however, some improvements in NO_x emissions should result. The inspection-maintenance system strategy for Chicago and Cook County provides an emission reduction of six percent for CO and 6.8 percent for HC. This is an additional reduction over the Chicago inspection-maintenance of only 0.5 percent for CO and 0.6 percent for HC.

The strategy extended to a three county area yields a total reduction of 6.2 percent for CO and 7.0 percent for HC. The additional improvement is extremely small and constitutes an almost imperceptible change in the carbon monoxide levels. Even less of a change is brought about by the extension of the system to the entire six county SMSA. The additional percentage reductions are only 0.07 percent for CO and 0.07 percent for HC in the CBD over and above the three county system.

The reduction in emissions estimated over the entire SMSA, rather than just within the CBD, will of course be substantially higher. If the percentage reduction over the entire SMSA is assumed to be proportional to the reduction in the emission factors for private automobiles (the vast majority of traffic in the area) then a 30 percent reduction in CO and a 40 percent reduction in HC would result. The evaluation of the advisability of extending inspection-maintenance systems to larger geographical areas, therefore, is dependent on the goal for which the sytem is being developed. If the goal is to reduce emissions in the CBD, extensions of the system beyond Chicago appear questionable.

Inspection-Maintenance Costs

Four cost components are calculated for inspection-maintenance. These are (1) administrative inspection costs, (2) extra maintenance costs, (3) waiting time costs and (4) fuel savings. Costs are expressed in terms of the 1975 present value costs of a program operating from 1975 through 1980. A discount rate of six percent is used. This approach yields figures which may be regarded as the amount that one would have to invest in 1975 at six percent to cover all costs for a six year period.

Administrative Costs.   The annual administrative cost of inspection is based on the following formula:

$$CI = Cvt \; \frac{12}{M} (1 + F) \tag{3-2}$$

where:

CI =   annual average inspection cost per vehicle,

Cvt =   inspection cost per vehicle test,

F =   rejection rate (percentage of vehicles failing the test and requiring another one), and

M =   inspection interval in months.

Thus, total annual inspection cost is $V(CI)$ where V is the number of vehicles inspected.

Administrative inspection cost estimates per vehicle have been made by a number of groups: Northrup [16], the federal EPA [8], Chicago's Department of Environmental Control [5] and TRW [9]. Estimates of inspection costs from Chicago's Department of Environmental Control are employed here although these costs are considerably higher than those from the other studies. Initial capital costs of approximately $6 million will be incurred to start the system.[5] Operating costs are expected to stabilize at about $3 million per year or about $2.27 per vehicle. This is a little more than twice as high as the EPA estimates. The total administrative costs for the four alternative systems are shown in Table 3-3.

Extra Maintenance. In addition to the inspection costs there are costs of extra emission-related maintenance. This consists of the cost of diagnosis plus the costs of repairs. This cost is the difference between total costs of maintenance which incur with an inspection system and the previous total costs of maintenance which arose voluntarily.

Extra annual maintenance costs can be calculated using the following formula:

$$VC_m = \left[F(\frac{12}{M} Cem) - F[\frac{12}{MIF}(Ccm)] \right] \tag{3-3}$$

where:

C_m = annual total cost for emission-related maintenance,

M = inspection interval in months,

MIF = current average maintenance interval of vehicles failing inspection test in months,

F = rejection rate,

Cem = cost per vehicle service event for emission-related maintenance,

Ccm = cost per vehicle service event for present conventional maintenance, and

V = the number of vehicles taking the test in each of the i years.

Maintenance costs for cars rejected (Cem) were studied by the federal

Table 3-3. **Administrative Inspection Costs 30 Percent Rejection Rate (millions of dollars)**

	Cost for 1975	Present Value 1975–1980 (Six percent Discount)
Chicago	3.0	15.2
Cook County	6.4	33.3
Three Counties	8.1	43.9
SMSA	9.1	49.0

Table 3-4. Extra Maintenance Costs 30 Percent Rejection Rate (millions of dollars)

	Cost for 1975	*Present Value 1975-1980 (Six percent Discount)*
Chicago	1.66	8.4
Cook County	3.48	18.1
Three Counties	4.47	24.2
SMSA	5.05	27.2

EPA [8], Northrup [17], New Jersey [4] and Clayton Manufacturing Company [20]. An EPA estimate of $25.00 cost per serviced vehicle is used here. A study of owner maintenance habits indicates that the average cost per vehicle service event (*Cem*) for present conventional vehicles is about $36.00. This survey also found that 30 percent of the vehicle population has a maintenance interval of greater than 12 months. For this group, the average length of the interval is 22 months.

If the premise is accepted that vehicles which are presently serviced at least once every 12 months pass the inspection screening, then only that group of vehicles which is serviced less frequently will bear additional maintenance costs. The great majority of rejected vehicles which will require extra maintenance should fall into the 30 percent category. Thus, an estimate for the current average maintenance interval of vehicles failing inspection (*MIF*) is 22 months. Using this data in the above formula, the maintenance costs were calculated and are presented in Table 3-4.

Gasoline Savings. If inspection-maintenance is successful in reducing emissions, it should theoretically also result in gasoline savings.[1] The proper estimate of net gasoline savings from inspection systems is the difference between those total fuel savings which result from the maintenance required by inspection systems and those total savings realized from

---

1. Theoretical gasoline savings in grams per mile are: GPM = 0.3 CO + 1.0 HC, where CO and HC are the reductions in these pollutants in grams per mile. The results thus obtained should be multiplied by 0.67 to account for deterioration of effects over the year.

In theory the savings from use of an Idle Mode test, S_1, would be $21.57 with gasoline priced at 60 cents per gallon. A problem which arises is that considerable discrepancy exists between theoretical and measured savings.[6, 20] Most of this discrepancy is due to a fairly small number of vehicles which show atypical results. When atypical vehicles are eliminated from the experimental results, the figures are fairly close to the theoretical values.[6,20] The question is whether these results are due to known difficulties in measurement or whether they represent real phenomena that will appear in actual programs. The figures for gasoline savings used here are lower than theoretical results and conform to some experimental results although they are higher than some others.

Table 3-5.   Gasoline Savings 30 Percent Rejection Rate
(millions of dollars) Idle Mode

	1975 Estimates	Present Value 1975-1980 (Six percent Discount)
Chicago	2.85	15.0
Cook County	6.54	34.4
Three Counties	8.15	42.9
SMSA	9.14	48.1

normal tuneup. The savings is calculated by:

$$S = F \left[\frac{12}{I} s_1 - \frac{12}{M} s_2 \right] \qquad\qquad (3\text{-}4)$$

where:

F =   rejection rate,

I =   inspection interval in months,

s_1 =   gasoline savings per serviced vehicle for emission-related maintenance schedule,

s_2 =   gasoline savings which would have been realized by the failed vehicle from its normal tuneup schedule,

M =   current average maintenance interval for failed vehicles in months, and

S =   saving per vehicle per year.

EPA reports a figure which when adjusted to a 60 cents per gallon gasoline price yields a value for S_1 of \$14.60 per car rejected by the Idle Mode test. It is also assumed that gasoline prices increase by two percent per year. No good estimates exist for S_2, the savings attainable from normal tuneup. These may not be large since engine parameters which maximize engine smoothness do not minimize emissions or gasoline savings. It is arbitrarily assumed that S_1 is equal to $0.5S_2$. This, however, is quite probably high and results in a conservative estimate of gasoline savings. The final results are extremely sensitive to the parameters determining gasoline savings and this should be borne in mind when viewing the results.

Waiting Time.   One important cost of the inspection-maintenance system involves waiting time for inspection. Waiting time costs are calculated by:

$$T.C. = \sum_{i=1}^{T} W[N_o (1+g)^i] [Y(1+p)^i] [1+F] [1+r]^{-i} \qquad (3\text{-}5)$$

where:

N = number of cars,

W = waiting time,

Y = after tax wage income,

F = rejection rate,

i = each of the i years from 1975 to 1980,

g and p = growth rates for W and Y respectively, and

r = discount rate.

Guttman indicates that a figure near the after tax wage is representative of waiting time costs.[12] This rate is assumed to be 75 percent of the before tax wage. On this basis, Chicago wages would be $3.93 per hour in 1975. These figures are conservative since automobile drivers as a whole earn above average incomes. Evidence is that a waiting time of 20 minutes per car is quite reasonable.[5] These waiting time costs are shown in Table 3-6.

Summary of Inspection-Maintenance Costs and Effectiveness.
Table 3-7 presents the total costs and effectiveness of the inspection-maintenance Idle Mode system in terms of the present value of a six year program beginning in 1975. The resulting estimate of costs is equivalent to a total charge per vehicle of $3.68. This estimate is, however, quite sensitive to the gasoline cost savings, which are considered to be conservative. Actual costs of the program could be drastically reduced if gasoline prices went to $1 a gallon or more optimistic fuel savings estimates were employed.

Table 3-6. Waiting Time Cost 30 Percent Rejection Rate (millions of dollars)

	Waiting Cost 1975	*Present Value 1975–1980 (Six percent Discount)*
Chicago	1.1	5.7
Cook County	2.2	12.3
Three Counties	2.7	15.7
SMSA	3.0	17.0

Table 3–7.   **Summary of Inspection-Maintenance Cost and Effectiveness Idle Mode**

	Present Value 1975–1980 (Millions of Dollars)	*Percent Reduction in CO*	*Pollution HC*
Chicago	44.3	5.5	6.2
Cook County	98.1	6.0	6.8
Three Counties	126.7	6.2	7.0
SMSA	141.3	6.27	7.07

It can be readily seen that the cost-effectiveness ratio rises quite rapidly as the inspection is extended to larger areas. The ratio in terms of dollars per percentage reduction in CO rises from about $8 million for Chicago to about $23 million for the SMSA. A similar situation exists for HC. The incremental cost per additional percent reduction increases even more dramatically. Clearly, in terms of a localized pollution control policy for the CBD, the conclusion is that the inspection system should be specified in the smallest political jurisdictional area which contains the CBD. In subsequent comparisons of the inspection-maintenance system with other CBD control policies, only the system involving city-registered cars will be considered in view of its evident superiority.

In terms of its feasibility as a control policy the acceptance of an inspection-maintenance system by the motoring public has not been fully demonstrated. If long waiting times and involved administrative procedures become prevalent, the systems could meet with public opposition. Another possible implementation difficulty, which was observed in the design and operation of the New Jersey inspection system, is the lack of adequate servicing facilities and trained personnel to absorb the expected number of rejected vehicles requiring tuneups. Present facilities in most cities may not be able to support a rejection rate greater than about 20 percent. Especially with the additional demand, maintenance costs may run unnecessarily high and this could also lead to public opposition. The development of inspection-related services aimed only at passing the inspection but not at reducing emissions is another possibility. These potential defects must be carefully evaluated in considering adoption of a program.

The appropriate testing regime must also be considered in setting up a program. Most jurisdictions have adopted the Idle Mode test, the one evaluated here. However, the popularity of this test is not warranted. The decision as to which testing regime to adopt is a key decision. Two of the alternative testing regimes merit attention: engine parameter tests and emission tests at key modes. The more sophisticated the testing regime the greater the reduction in emissions, but equipment and waiting time costs are higher. Annual per car differences in capital and operating costs between the Idle and Key

Mode tests come to about 25 cents per car per year.[1, 3, 4, 9, 15, 18] For
Chicago this would amount to over $250,000 per year. Waiting time costs
are also greater. The Key Mode test requires about five minutes per test as
compared with two minutes per test for the Idle Mode test.

These additional costs must be weighed against the savings from
better gasoline mileage. The fuel economy is due to more efficient combustion
resulting from more sophisticated automotive diagnoses. The interpretation
of the exact gasoline savings figures is a complex matter.[1, 3, 6, 20] The
extent of the fuel savings is highly correlated with emission reductions. For
tests performed in California and Michigan our calculations indicate that for
measured differences in gasoline savings the superior gasoline savings of the
Key Mode as compared with the Idle Mode more than offset the higher equipment costs and waiting time costs associated with the Key Mode. The Key
Mode may in fact produce savings sufficient to give this strategy negative costs.
This, of course, is an important finding. The justification for investment in
sophisticated diagnostic systems is that emission reductions are highly correlated
with fuel economy.

Why have most jurisdictions adopted the Idle Mode test? The
justifications suggested here are first, that since the equipment costs are less
for the Idle Mode regime the jurisdictions' own costs are less and the jurisdiction is apt to be more sensitive to its own costs than the costs imposed on
others; and second, appreciation of the fuel savings was not general at the time
the Idle Mode test was adopted in some localities. Ultimately, the justification
of sophisticated automobile diagnostic testing may lie as much in its possible
fuel savings as in its environmental effects.

TRAFFIC FLOW STRATEGIES

Traffic flow strategies designed to increase average speeds and thereby reduce
emissions are the second set of local pollution strategies to be examined. These
are by their very nature highly localized in their impact. The design of such
strategies is closely linked to the concerns of traffic engineering—i.e., roadway
configuration, lane widths, traffic signalization, parking controls, etc. Two
types of traffic flow improvement strategies are considered for evaluation here:
the improvement of traffic speeds in the CBD by improved traffic signal systems,
and the total banning of on-street parking in the CBD area.

Improved Signals
The speed of flow of traffic in downtown areas is in large part
determined by the delays caused at closely spaced intersections. Each intersection will normally have some form of signal to regulate traffic flows. In
Chicago and almost all other major cities such signals usually take the form of
lights with fixed timing for green-yellow-red cycles. Once the cycle time has

been set, further adjustments to the signal cycle are made only at infrequent intervals. The difficulty with such signal systems is that traffic volumes can vary greatly over different seasons or even during a single day. There exists no single optimal cycle time for intersection signals which will yield the best traffic flow conditions under all of the possible traffic demand conditions on a downtown street.

As an alternative to such fixed time systems several cities have installed, or are proposing to install, a computerized traffic signal system which allows cycle times to be altered in response to traffic demand changes. Essentially, these systems consist of three components: detectors, controllers and a computer. Detectors are buried beneath crucial intersections and have the task of relaying information about vehicle flow to a computer. With this information the computer analyzes the traffic situation and then sends impulses to the controllers, which in turn activate traffic signals. The computer-induced impulses alter signal timing cycles so that traffic flow is maximized.

Stanford Research Institute (SRI) made a study of the effects of the introduction of such a computerized system on vehicular speeds in downtown Chicago.[23] A simulation model was employed which accounted for the effects of different traffic demands for CBD streets, street capacities and the cumulative delays in traffic flow caused by closely spaced intersection signals. Both the present and projected computerized signal systems were evaluated in terms of overall speed increases.

The SRI study indicated that traffic flow improvements would increase speeds by 22 percent.[21] Emissions were computed based on emission factors modified for this speed correction. These emission factors were then applied to projected vehicular miles of travel in the area. Using this approach, emission reductions due to the speed increases are 6.1 percent for CO and 5.5 percent for HC. Since the strategy results in higher average route speeds, there is a small (2.9 percent) increase in nitrogen oxide emissions.

Cost estimates for the computer-controlled system include a procurement cost per intersection of $18,000 and an annual operation and maintenance cost per intersection of $250.[21] Assuming a system service life of 15 years, total present value cost can be computed.

$$\text{Present worth total cost} = C_{pw} = C_1 + OM\left[\frac{(1+r)^n - 1}{r(1+r)^n}\right] \tag{3.6}$$

where:

C_1 = procurement cost per intersection times the number of intersections,

OM = operation and maintenance costs per intersection times number of intersections,

$\Big[\quad\Big]$ = capital recovery factor,

r = interest rate, and

n = service life of project.

This produces a figure of $1.504 million for the computer-controlled system. Other required improvements to existing intersection controls would add another $1 million. Comparison of these cost estimates for the computerized control system with actual costs which other cities have incurred indicates that the $2.504 million figure is a generous estimate of the costs.

The cost-effectiveness ratio for this program, again in terms of dollars per percent reduction, is $.33 million per percent reduction of CO. Approximately the same figure applies to HC. These figures, however, are in a sense misleading if compared directly to the cost-effectiveness ratio of a local pollution policy, such as inspection-maintenance, whose sole purpose is to reduce emissions. Traffic signal improvements, in the case of Chicago and many other major cities, may pay for themselves in terms of reducing congestion and travel time. The incremental cost of a computerized traffic signal system as a pollution control measure for many major cities is thus zero. Only in areas where such systems cannot be justified solely on traffic congestion grounds, but might be adopted on the basis of pollution control effects, can costs be properly ascribed to computerized controls as an emission control policy.

There is some evidence that measures taken to increase traffic flow work only temporarily by themselves. Increases in traffic flow stimulate a latent trip demand and increase the volume of traffic until all speeds are reduced. The counterargument to this is that the number of automobile trips is essentially limited by the number of parking spaces in the CBD so that, with a given number of parking spaces, speed increases can be maintained. With regard to latent trip demand, a recent EPA study noted that:[10]

> . . . from a pollution viewpoint, both long term traffic trends and induced travel tend to limit the air pollution control potential of traffic flow improvements in the medium and long term period. In most metropolitan areas, the additional capacity afforded by traffic flow improvements would tend to be used up within 2 to 4 years because of the higher volume which would be attracted.
>
> Travel induced by substantial traffic flow improvements (i.e., far greater than the present levels of highway and street improvements programs) could contribute an additional amount of growth in the downtown street network as latent demand is activated. These higher growth rates, of course, could consume additional capacity even more rapidly.

On-Street Parking Restrictions

The evaluation of the emission reductions resulting from the implementation of a ban of on-street parking is extremely difficult. There is no question that on-street parking affects traffic flow conditions in the CBD to a considerable extent by restricting lane widths and thereby reducing street capacity. The evaluation of the effects of banning on-street parking or standing of vehicles is complicated by the very nature of the commercial activities required in the downtown area. Due to the concentration of commercial and retail activities in the CBD, much of the traffic in this area is of a circulatory nature with a large percentage of vehicle trips for the purpose of making deliveries or short-term transactional business. Further complicating the traffic flow in the area is the large amount of pedestrian traffic generated by the commercial and retail interests. In the case of Chicago, volumes of up to 80,000 pedestrians per block per hour have been estimated in the CBD. These factors complicate CBD traffic patterns and make it difficult to evaluate the effects of parking bans.

There are several empirical indications of the air quality improvement that may be obtained from parking bans. Many cities in Europe and in the United States have attempted experiments in partial or total traffic bans in certain areas of their central commercial districts to ascertain the air quality and congestion effects of such measures. The results of these traffic experiments reported by Orski indicate dramatic improvements in air quality.[17] For example, in Marseilles, France a limited traffic ban was imposed for ten days in October, 1970 in order to ascertain the air quality effects in certain areas of the city. Readings of 18.8 parts per million of carbon monoxide were recorded before this experiment. During the traffic ban experiments, 502 air quality samples were taken at two hour intervals and it was found that the concentration of carbon monoxide was reduced to 11.6 parts per million, approximately a 33 percent reduction in carbon monoxide concentration. Similarly significant results were obtained in Tokyo, Japan and Bremen, Germany.

The method of calculating the percentage reductions of pollutants in this study is to estimate the increase in capacity of CBD streets as a result of the ban on parking, and then to relate this increase in capacity to an increase in speed which could be effected under the given parking ban proposal. Once an average speed increase is known, the emission reductions can be calculated by adjusting the emission factors.

The increase in capacity of downtown streets is measured in terms of the increase in capacity of their signal-equipped intersections. This practice is consistent with the philosophy employed in the Stanford Research Institute traffic study [23] and with present traffic flow planning. Generally speaking, the capacity of urban arterials which are reasonably well controlled by traffic lights will be dependent upon the intersection along the arterial with the highest traffic demand. For the purpose of estimating a capacity increase due to the ban on parking, it was assumed that the average major arterial in the CBD of Chicago was approximately 60 feet in width and was presently operating at capacity. Average conditions with respect to percentage of turning traffic, trucks and buses at its intersections were also assumed. Under these conditions the change in capacity of the arterial or of its intersection with the highest traffic volume can be calculated using traffic engineering performance relationships presented in the *Highway Capacity Manual.* [13] It should be noted that these assumptions will at best only yield approximate estimations of the capacity increases effected by the parking ban proposals.

Since the traffic effects of a ban of on-street parking will vary for one-way and two-way streets, the analysis must examine these cases separately. For the cases analyzed here it is assumed that parking is banned on one side of one-way streets and completely banned on two-way streets. For urban streets with one-way traffic and on-street parking, under the previously cited conditions, a 13 percent capacity improvement between the parking and no parking conditions for one-way streets was estimated. A similar calculation for two-way streets indicated approximately a 50 percent increase in capacity if on-street parking is banned.

These increases in capacity are transformed into changes in vehicle speed on the basis of capacity-speed relationships. Empirical studies have shown that as a traffic volume to roadway capacity ratio falls, the speed of traffic increases. Utilizing empirical relationships between volume-capacity ratios and overall average travel speeds on urban streets as presented in the *Highway Capacity Manual,* the above capacity increases will yield approximately a 13 percent increase in speed on one-way streets if parking is banned on one-way streets, and a 21 percent increase in speed on two-way streets if parking is banned on two-way streets. Applying the ratio of one-way streets to total streets in the CBD yields a weighted average speed increase of 16.0 percent for the complete banning of on-street parking within the CBD.

This procedure shows that a parking ban under investigation results in a 6.3 percent reduction of CO. For HC there was a 5.4 percent reduction, while for NO_x there was a 0.5 percent increase. It should be emphasized that any of the above estimation techniques must be viewed critically in terms of the amount of data available for making such an estimation, particularly in the area of the speed improvement calculation and also with respect to the complexity of the factors affecting traffic flow within the CBD.

The economic costs associated with a partial or total ban of on-street parking in the CBD are extremely difficult to estimate quantitatively. Such a ban would affect several types of vehicular trips in the CBD, and the severity of the effect of the ban would greatly differ depending on which trip types were being discussed. For those shoppers and businessmen who presently use street parking as more convenient than off-street parking facilities, an estimate of the cost of this policy might be made by assessing the increased costs in parking charges and walking times for these on-street parkers. The effect of the parking ban would be to increase the parking cost of even the shortest trip into the CBD area to the minimum one-half hour parking fee. In order to make an estimate of the total cost of this policy with respect to on-street automobile parking, it would be necessary to have some knowledge of the distribution of off-street parking times. This type of cost calculation excludes the cost to the CBD commercial interests entailed in the diversion of shopping and commercial business from the CBD to other areas of the region because of decreased accessibility to the CBD. This diversion represents a transfer of revenue from the CBD to other commercial locations and for the most part is not a cost in the strict sense. However, the effects on the commercial viability of the CBD of decreasing access to commercial interests are certainly a factor which should be carefully weighed in evaluating the on-street parking ban proposals.

A second type of vehicle trip affected by the on-street parking ban is deliveries to CBD stores and restaurants. Without the implementation of a nighttime delivery policy, it is difficult to determine how the commercial interests in the CBD area could properly be serviced by commercial delivery vehicles at the present volume without some form of on-street standing or parking. The costs of nighttime delivery operations are discussed in a later section.

Due to the difficulties of estimating the cost of this policy, no cost-effectiveness ratios were computed. The emission reductions from parking bans are almost equivalent to those generated because of improved signal systems. If the emission estimation techniques employed here are reliable, the cost-effectiveness ratio of improved signals would be less than that of an on-street parking ban due to the fact that the traffic signal policy is not commercially disruptive. Thus, in terms of traffic flow improvement strategies the computerized signal system alternative would seem to be a dominant policy option in highly congested CBD situations. In later comparisons with other local emission control policies only traffic signal improvement will be considered.

TAXI CONTROLS

The relatively high percentage of pollution emissions in the CBD caused by taxi fleet operations raises the possibility of a third policy option: namely, that increased controls on taxis in addition to those required by the new car standards may constitute an effective method of improving air quality in central city areas. Although taxi emission contributions will fall rapidly as new car standards are enforced, the high CBD pollution contributions per taxi due to their intensive use in the central city area suggest that even further controls placed on the relatively few vehicles in taxi fleets will have a disproportionate effect in reducing emissions.

Two alternative taxi strategies are considered in this section: the conversion of taxis to fuels with low emission characteristics, specifically propane (LPG); and the retrofitting of in-use taxis with more stringent emission control devices than those required for private cars. The conversion of taxis to propane fuels requires the installation of propane fuel tanks and alterations in the taxi fuel feed systems. Retrofitting of taxis requires that all taxis be fitted with catalytic mufflers or emission controls of equal efficiency. Both of these strategies augment the effect of the new car standards so as to reduce the emissions of the total taxi fleet operations to a minimum in as short a time as possible. These strategies were assumed to affect only the emission in the CBD area to any significant extent since the bulk of taxi use is in and around this area.

Emission Effects
For the taxi strategies involving the conversion to LPG, a new weighted emission factor was computed based on adjustments of the emission factor formula (Equation 2-1) given in Chapter Two. The emission factor for taxis was modified to reflect current estimates of LPG emission rates.[8, 14] The following emission factors were applied to all propane fueled vehicles:

3.4 grams per mile carbon monoxide
0.67 grams per mile hydrocarbons
2.8 grams per mile nitrogen oxides.

The new weighted emission factor was applied to the 22 percent of the vehicle miles traveled in the Chicago CBD attributable to taxis. Assuming a complete conversion of the taxi fleet, an 8.5 percent reduction in CO, a 7.5 percent reduction in HC and a 0.3 percent reduction in NO_x are achievable.

The emission reductions resulting from a strategy requiring catalytic converter retrofit were calculated in a similar manner. The emission factor for taxis assumed in this case utilized the 1980 emission factors for that class of vehicles (1.97 grams per mile CO, 0.73 grams per mile HC and 0.8 grams per mile NO_x). With a total fleet retrofit strategy the following emission reductions are forecast: 10 percent CO, 7.2 percent HC and 3.6 percent NO_x.

Liquid Propane Conversion Cost
The costs of converting all or part of the Chicago taxi fleet to LPG programs consist of (1) capital costs of conversion, (2) fuel costs, (3) costs of refueling facilities and (4) maintenance costs. These costs are lower for taxis which are manufactured to run on LPG or similar fuels than for taxis made to run on gasoline which are converted to use LPG. All calculations are made for the conversion case in which costs are higher.[14]

The costs of converting to LPG are very sensitive to fuel costs and mileage obtained. Differences in taxes between LPG and gasoline could result in considerable differences in conversion costs. These tax costs would be costs to the taxi companies, however, and not costs to society. Correct social costs are found by using fuel costs net of taxes.

A large number of mileage estimates for LPG- and gasoline-powered vehicles appear in the literature.[4] A reasonable estimate is that gasoline-powered cabs get 10.5 miles per gallon and LPG-powered cabs obtain 8.3 miles to the gallon. The mileage associated with later model gasoline-powered automobiles is expected to decline by five percent to ten percent because of pollution control measures. This means that for pre–1975 cars, LPG fuel costs are about equivalent to gasoline costs, but that in later years there is a definite advantage with LPG.

The total of the various costs in 1975 for the complete conversion of taxis to propane is $1.9 million. The present values of these programs discounted at six percent from 1975 to 1980 respectively is $0.84 million. The present value costs are lower for the whole six year period than for 1975 alone because of the fuel savings over the six year period. However, as was pointed out, this figure is quite sensitive to the relative prices of gas and LPG.

Retrofit Costs

The cost of retrofitting in-use taxis is composed of the capital and installation cost of the catalytic converter device, the maintenance cost for the converter and the cost of extra fuel. The capital costs of retrofitting vary with the age of the vehicle, as do the fuel penalties. Maintenance costs consist of catalyst replacement.

Data concerning the age distribution of taxis and annual miles traveled were obtained from interviews with the large taxi companies and from work by Kitch.[15] The capital cost estimates are based on actual bid figures submitted by several manufacturing companies. The necessary retrofit unit costs by vehicle age are shown in Table 3–8.

In accordance with the information on the age distribution of taxis it is assumed that one-fourth of the taxi fleet is replaced each year. It is proper to assume that the pollution control costs for new cars in 1976 and thereafter

Table 3-8. Taxi Retrofit Costs

Capital Costs	Additional Operational Costs	Additional Car Maintenance Costs
$250 for pre-1975 cars	1% fuel penalty plus 2.5% higher prices for non-leaded gasoline	$30 per 50,000 miles
$140 per car after 1972		

are not properly attributed to the retrofit policy since these vehicles will be controlled by new car standards. For the retrofit of the entire taxi fleet the operating and maintenance costs are incurred for three-fourths of the fleet in 1976, for half of the fleet in 1977, and for one-fourth of the fleet in 1978. No costs are incurred thereafter.

A comparison of the cost-effectiveness of the retrofit policy with the LPG conversion would seem to indicate a slight superiority in favor of retrofitting. For LPG conversion a cost-effectiveness of $1.9 million per 8.5 percent reduction of CO is compared to $1.5 million for a 10 percent reduction of CO with the retrofitting program. Similar calculations hold for HC, and a more pronounced advantage in favor of retrofitting occurs for the control of the oxides of nitrogen. Consequently, in later discussions only the taxi retrofit program will be considered due to its superior performance. It should be noted, however, that the objections raised to the use of catalytic mufflers in Chapter Two may also be raised in regard to the retrofitting strategy. Thus, the cost-effective advantage of retrofit is in terms of reductions in regulated pollutants only and does not account for unregulated emissions effects. In addition, this superiority is sensitive to the price and availability of LPG. With lower LPG prices and greater availability, conversion to LPG can become quite attractive.

TRUCK STRATEGIES

The final class of local control policy options to be evaluated considers changes in freight operations in the CBD. The increasing importance of freight vehicular activity as a source of air pollution in the central business district was noted. By 1975 truck activity in the Chicago CBD will account for approximately one-quarter of the emissions of carbon monoxide, 28 percent of the emissions of hydrocarbons and 10 percent of nitrogen oxides. In the case of carbon monoxides and hydrocarbons, this represents about a 10 percent increase in the percentage contribution of these pollutants from 1971 to 1975. This increase is due mainly to the reduction in pollution levels associated with other automotive traffic, without a concomitant reduction in the emission rates associated with truck activity. In 1977 the situation becomes even more dramatic and trucks and trucking activity account for about 40 percent of the emissions of carbon monoxide and hydrocarbons. This is roughly equivalent to the emissions of private passenger cars in that year.

Two strategies aimed at reducing the emissions from truck activities within the central business district will be investigated. The first strategy focuses on the truck vehicle itself and considers the retrofitting of emission control devices on trucks or the conversion of trucks operating in the central business district to liquid propane fuel. This strategy is equivalent to the one discussed with regard to taxis and seeks to reduce emissions by reducing the emission rate of trucks per vehicle miles of travel. The second strategy is the rescheduling of truck deliveries to nighttime hours. The rationale for such a policy lies in the fact that all violations of federal air quality standards normally occur within the daytime hours within the central business district. The shifting of a portion of the emissions from daytime to nighttime reduces the overall daytime emission level in the central city and thereby improves air quality. The total mass of emissions remains constant under this policy but altering the time of occurrence of a significant portion of truck emissions allows for a more thorough dispersion of pollutants and a lower air pollutant concentration.

Retrofit and Liquid Propane Fuel Conversions

The LPG strategy assumes that all trucks operating in the CBD are converted to use this fuel. Emission factors for LPG converted trucks are:

4.2 grams per mile carbon monoxide
2.4 grams per mile hydrocarbons
2.8 grams per mile nitrogen oxides

The above emission factors were substituted for the truck category and new overall weighted emission factors computed and applied using the same methodology described in Chapter Two.

The potential effectiveness of truck controls is quite impressive. At 100 percent conversion of the truck fleet to LPG there is a 26 percent reduction of CO, a 25.4 percent reduction in HC, and a 7.0 percent reduction in NO_x. The significance of the reduction is magnified in the years after 1975 when the percentage of emissions associated with freight deliveries increases from 20 to 40 percent.

As an alternative to truck LPG conversion, retrofit of intercity trucks may be considered. At present, the costs of truck retrofit are high, since operating problems have yet to be completely worked out. However, the city of New York is experimenting with heavy duty gasoline truck retrofit systems using catalytic converters, and indications are that the retrofit costs will fall over time. Nevertheless, LPG conversion dominates the retrofit strategy and further retrofit calculations are unreported. If a retrofit strategy were implemented, the emission factors and emission reduction would be quite similar to those for the LPG conversion strategy.

Conversion to LPG has already been undertaken by some trucking companies because of economies offered by LPG. The most important variable in the calculations of the total cost of conversions, and the one for which it is most difficult to obtain accurate information, is the number of trucks operating in the CBD. An estimate of 7000 trucks operating daily in the Chicago CBD may be made from traffic count figures.

Conversion costs are estimated to be $600 per vehicle, and additional fueling facilities to be $17 per truck per year.[7] Fuel costs are important, yet difficult to estimate. The best available evidence is that mileage for gasoline-powered cars is about 25 percent better than for LPG-powered cars. Indications are, however, that the larger the engine, the less the fuel penalty for use on LPG. Maintenance costs are estimated here to be $50 less per truck per year with use of LPG rather than gasoline. Costs for conversion of CBD trucks to LPG based on the above data are shown in Table 3-9.

Nighttime Delivery of Freight

The specific form of freight rescheduling investigated here involves the shifting of freight delivery operations from the present daytime delivery to one which would begin at 1:00 P.M. and extend to 10:00 P.M. In examinations of the diurnal pattern of freight deliveries within the central cities it was found that the hours of 10:00 A.M. and 2:00 P.M. presently constitute the peak times for freight deliveries in central cities. This corresponds with the pattern of peak truck delivery activity. It is assumed that regulations forbidding the delivery of freight in the morning hours would shift the peak delivery periods to 3:00 P.M. and 8:00 P.M.

The daytime hours are critical with respect to the criteria for the attainment of federal air quality standards. Assuming that 50 percent of the present activity of delivery vehicles takes place after normal commercial hours, the emission reduction associated with this strategy is simply one-half of the emissions due to delivery truck operations in the CBD. The percentage of contributions to emissions from different vehicle classes is obtained from Figure 3-1 in Chapter Three. The 1975 emission reductions due to nighttime rescheduling of deliveries are found to be 13.6 percent for carbon monoxide, 14.4 percent for hydrocarbons and 5.3 percent for nitrogen oxide.

Interestingly, the reductions in emissions due to either the rescheduling of deliveries or the conversion of delivery trucks from gasoline to liquid propane cause a greater percentage reduction than any other local emission control strategy. Reductions due to nighttime delivery regulations, like those of the truck propane conversion program, become more effective in the period beyond 1975 as trucks become the cause of a greater percentage of the emissions generated within the central business district.

The cost of a system of nighttime delivery must be calculated with

Table 3-9. Costs of Conversion of CBD Trucks to LPG

Present value, 1975 for 1975-1980 period	*Annual Costs of a six year program at six percent*
$4,710,000	$958,000

respect to the costs incurred both by the trucking firms and by the customers receiving the shipments. In order to estimate the additional cost to the trucking firms making deliveries, some estimate of the present freight bill for CBD deliveries is required. These costs will consist of driver cost and vehicle costs expressed on a dollar per vehicle mile basis for less than truckload deliveries in central city areas. The cost may be calculated by

$$TFC = VMT[C_L + C_T] \qquad\qquad (3\text{-}7)$$

where:

TFC = total freight bill,

VMT = vehicle miles traveled per year for freight delivery under congested conditions,

C_L = cost per vehicle miles of labor,

C_T = cost per vehicle mile associated with the use of trucks—i.e., maintenance, capital cost, licenses, etc.

Assuming an approximate estimate of 10,000 miles per year per driver and using the average wage rate reported for truck drivers, a unit cost per mile of about $1 for intercity delivery is appropriate.[26] The cost of truck operation was derived from the *Annual Motor Vehicle Report,* Government Service Administration 1972. By using a weighted average of the costs of operating light duty trucks (a majority of the CBD delivery fleet) and heavy duty vehicles, an average vehicular cost of 20 cents per mile was arrived at. The present freight bill for the deliveries (50 percent) affected by the nighttime delivery system is thus $12.6 million.

In order to estimate the additional costs to the trucking industry from a rescheduling, an estimate must be made regarding the increased wages necessary to induce drivers to work on a partial nighttime basis. A recent survey of union practices regarding nighttime premium payments indicates that the highest premium paid for nighttime deliveries is ten percent above the present wage rates.[26] This would, however, tend to be offset by the reduction in congestion costs due to truck operations at night. It has been estimated that up to 15 percent of a truck's time is spent unproductively due to inner city congestion. This will affect both the productivity of the truck and the driver. For the purposes of this calculation, an overall increase in productivity of 15 percent was applied to those vehicle miles assumed to be shifted to nighttime. Thus, when one-half of the delivery is made at night the freight bill can be re-estimated as:

$$TFC[\text{night}] = .50 VMT \cdot (1 - .15) [1.10C_L + C_T].\tag{3-8}$$

This yields an estimate of $11.6 million for nighttime deliveries which constitutes an actual saving of $1 million.

The estimate of the cost to shipping customers consists mainly of the nighttime premiums paid to employees required to be on hand at the time of delivery. The average wages of warehousemen are equivalent to those of truck drivers and are estimated at approximately $11,000 per year.[26] Partial nighttime shifts will be required for warehousing or commercial personnel only on those days when a shipment is expected. Assuming a nighttime minimum store personnel requirement of two warehousemen, the additional yearly cost to freight receivers would be approximately $19,250,000 above present freight delivery costs. No offsetting increases in productivity are evident for the freight receivers. Net costs are thus on the order of $18 million per year.

In view of the high cost of nighttime delivery systems to freight receivers it must be concluded that conversion to LPG or retrofitting of control devices on trucks constitute superior control options. On an annual basis, the cost-effectiveness of LPG conversions perform over twice as well as nighttime delivery systems. This situation would change drastically, of course, if some method were found to make nighttime deliveries without store personnel being present. Such systems have been used in nighttime food delivery systems in which deliveries are stored overnight in locked security areas. In this type of arrangement nighttime deliveries in central areas could pay for themselves in terms of trucking company savings. But until such a system can be developed for central city areas, LPG conversion or retrofit constitute superior truck emission controls. Since retrofitting of trucks is still in an experimental stage, and its costs are uncertain, an LPG conversion policy is chosen as the most feasible and cost-effective of the truck strategies evaluated.

STAGGERING COMMERCIAL HOURS

The possibility of staggering working hours for commercial activities in the central business district was not extensively investigated since indications were that such strategies would not be effective. The basic problem in reducing emissions in the CBD by shifting commuter traffic is that the cause of high eight hour pollution averages is the constantly high noncommuter vehicular traffic in the CBD. An examination of Figure 1-3 shows that this high level of traffic for over ten hours is reflected in the air quality reading. Staggering the hours of commercial establishments for one or two hours is not a significant enough shift in diurnal emission patterns to allow a significantly greater dispersion of pollutants to take place. Shifting commuter traffic one hour earlier or later would have little effect on daily emissions; there would still be nine hours of peak volume traffic in the CBD. A commercial day of more than ten hours does not constitute a realistic air pollution control strategy and any shorter commercial day would not effectively dilute emissions during the peak hours.

COMPARISON OF LOCAL EMISSION
CONTROL ALTERNATIVES

From the various local strategies considered a rather strong preferential ranking of strategies emerges. Inspection systems for city-registered cars, a computerized traffic signal system, taxi retrofit and truck LPG conversion were superior strategies in each of these four categories respectively with regard to the overall objective of reducing local air quality violations. The effectiveness and present value costs of these strategies are indicated in Table 3-10.

Strictly in terms of the cost-effectiveness of reducing regulated pollutants in central areas, the strategies would be ranked in order of preference as truck conversion, taxi retrofit, traffic signal computerization and inspection-maintenance. Furthermore, there exists a significant enough difference in the cost-effective ratios to believe that this result is related more to the characteristics of CBD traffic patterns in general than to specific conditions in the Chicago CBD. Several qualifications of the validity of this ranking are in order. First, the cost estimates of inspection-maintenance seem to be substantially overstated if jurisdictions are willing to adopt the Key Mode instead of Idle Mode test, since gasoline savings are greatly increased under this form of testing.

A second qualification of some importance concerns the designation of the cost of computerizing traffic signals as a pollution control cost. Including congestion benefits produces a negative cost for this strategy. However, in the case of Chicago this sytem was going to be adopted regardless of possible pollution improvements and therefore its cost-effectiveness ratio is essentially zero (zero dollars per six percent reduction because costs are zero or negative). The direct costs of the system were designated as pollution control costs so that the costs of this strategy are clearly overstated.

A comparison of results for these local strategies, and for the federal new car standards and retrofit strategies described in Chapter Two,

Table 3-10. Comparison of Selected Local Strategies

| | *Reductions in Percentage* | | | *Present Value in* |
	CO	*HC*	*NO_x*	*1975 (millions)*
City Inspection (Idle Mode)	5.5	6.2	0	44.3
Traffic Signalization	6.1	5.5	-2.9	2.5
Taxi Retrofit (100%)	8.5	7.5	0.3	1.9
LPG Truck Conversion (100%)	26.0	25.0	7.0	4.0

show that the local strategies are considerably more cost-effective in reducing emissions in the central business district. The combined effects of local strategies will produce almost exactly the same reduction as that achieved by the new car standards. The importance of this can scarcely be overemphasized. These local control measures are several times less costly than the federal standards per percent reduction. Thus, this evaluation of local strategies to reduce pollution in problem areas re-emphasizes dramatically a point emphasized at the end of Chapter Two: There is a need for greater flexibility in program development in order to generate policies which reflect local air quality problems and which place a greater emphasis on the possibilities of local controls.

Chapter Four

Mass Transit as an Environmental Tool

OVERVIEW

The highest pollution level for those pollutants associated with transportation are found in city centers during or after periods of rush hour traffic. The potential of mass transit to reduce emissions of these pollutants arises precisely because mass transit is used most intensively for rush hour trips to the center of cities. The increased use of mass transit not only reduces pollution, but also lessens highway congestion, conserves fuel and reduces expenditures for highways and automobiles.

Although the purpose of this chapter is to provide a methodology for analyzing the relationship of mass transit to air pollution, these broader aspects of mass transit must be kept in mind. Indeed, many effects of mass transit are unrelated to pollution, and to evaluate the desirability of mass transit on this basis alone may be misleading. For example, the use of mass transit can affect highway congestion, which is an important consideration in its own right. More fundamentally, there is a strong relationship in cities between the strength of the mass transit system and the strength of the central business district so that questions of desirability of a central business district are intimately linked with questions of mass transit. This relationship raises difficult economic issues as well as issues related to the cultural and social life of the city.

The analysis here takes as given the existence of the mass transit system, and considers the extent to which changes in the patronage of the system affect pollution levels, and the associated costs of achieving these levels. The cost-effectiveness of mass transit is evaluated in a manner similar to other local strategies. A variety of mass transit strategies are investigated: (1) congestion tolls, (2) parking strategies, (3) fare changes and (4) exclusive bus lanes. Each of these in some way changes the relative travel time and cost associated with mass transit use. For each of the policies the effect on mass transit ridership and on automobile trips must be predicted. Also the costs associated with the policy must be calculated.

In order to predict the ridership, emission and cost changes of these policies, the use of a series of transportation and cost models is necessary. These include a modal split model, a highway congestion model, an emission model and a model of mass transit operating cost behavior. A modal split model determines the change in mass transit ridership, given changes in the relative costs, travel time and comfort of automobiles versus mass transit. This diversion of passengers to or from mass transit is then transformed into estimates of the total trips to the CBD by automobile, the change in vehicle miles traveled and the emissions generated. The costs of this diversion of traffic due to the policy under examination are of two types: (1) the change in mass transit costs due to increased or decreased patronage and (2) the change in travel costs on highways due to the change in automobile trips.

Mass transit strategies are more difficult to evaluate in terms of cost-effectiveness than either the federal programs or other local control strategies because of the requirements of relating transportation demand behavior to a final estimation of emission reductions. In the previous chapters, demand analysis did not play a significant role except for the automobile registration predictions. In evaluating mass transit strategies the demand for transportation services becomes critical.

In order to relate the requirements for transportation demand analysis to the evaluation of mass transit as a pollution control measure, the mechanism whereby mass transit incentives affect the behavior, cost and pollution associated with travel to the CBD by automobile must be understood. This involves an examination of supply and demand conditions of urban travel. To illustrate the important factors that affect these conditions a hypothetical urban mass transportation system will be examined. Let us assume that the total number of person trips to the CBD is fixed and that only two ways of traveling from a residential area to the CBD exist: a single freeway and a commuter train. The fare and travel time to commute by train are constant regardless of the number of people who use it. The travel time and operating cost of commuting by car, however, are affected by congestion: as volume increases, both the operating cost and travel time increase per vehicle mile. As total vehicle miles of automobile travel increase so also does the emission of pollutants in the CBD. If only travel time costs and vehicle related costs are relevant, traffic will increase on the highway until the congestion is such that the travel time and operating costs by automobile are equal to the fare costs and travel time costs by train. However, if traffic can be diverted from the congested road onto the commuter train, there would be a savings to society. Travel time by train would remain the same. Travel time on the highway would decrease due to the lower congestion so that the net travel savings of the diversion would be positive. Such savings are possible because the cost of road use perceived by an individual is different than for society. Individual users of highways do not consider the time costs they impose on other road users because of the congestion they create. In the case where both a freeway and a train service the CBD, the individual driver will make his decision to use one or the other based on his perceived cost of using the road or trains at the existing roadway volume. But if he chooses to use his automobile, the price of automobile travel to society includes not only his own travel costs but also the additional costs he imposes on all other road users.

The significance of the existence of congestion costs in evaluating mass transit incentives as an environmental tool is that measures which reduce congestion also reduce pollution. In terms of evaluating the cost-effectiveness of mass transit incentives, if the cost associated with such mass transit measures is actually a congestion savings then any pollution reductions are costless.

Transit incentives, in addition to resulting in congestion savings, may reduce the total expenditures of pollution control costs by eliminating the need for local control measures. Assume that the air quality in a hypothetical urban area is such that in order to meet air quality standards by a given date only a certain total volume of pollutants may be emitted per year from vehicular traffic. Since total emission is the product of an emission factor which reflects control device technology, and total vehicle miles traveled (VMT), the set of feasible combinations of emission factors and total VMT which meet a predetermined air quality standard may be depicted by the line ab in Figure 4-1. Point C represents the initial condition with respect to emission factors and VMT in the area. The policy question becomes, what combination of VMT reduction by means of mass transit incentives and emission factor reductions by means of control device application is most cost-effective.

If traffic can be reduced to V_1 it may be unnecessary to apply any additional control devices to cars to meet standards. As volumes rise, more stringent controls are necessary. Finally the volume of traffic (V_4) could become so great that controls effective enough to meet the standard would not

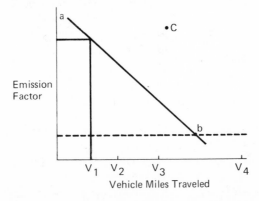

Figure 4-1. Emission Factors and Vehicle Miles Travelled.

exist. Mass transit incentives which reduce traffic from V_3 to, say, V_2 will lower the required emission factor reduction and the cost of pollution control per car. Theoretically traffic volume should be lowered until it reaches the point where additional savings in pollution control costs and congestion costs from a reduction in traffic volume are offset by the sum of the additional costs of substituting mass transit for private automobile use and the additional increased costs of carrying more riders on mass transit.

If the travel time cost of reducing traffic volumes is actually a saving due to the fact that roads are overcrowded from a social point of view, then such strategies may be quite cost-effective as pollution control measures. Congestion savings then become important in evaluating strategies to use mass transit for environmental improvement.

In the application of the methodology developed in this study, the pollution control cost saving of employing mass transit incentives as alternatives to other localized controls were not explicitly treated. This position was taken because travel and congestion costs in urban areas are orders of magnitude larger than the cost of many of the alternative pollution controls. Thus, the most significant cost elements in evaluating mass transit incentives as pollution control measures are not related to pollution but rather to the supply and demand conditions of the urban transportation system. The models and methodology presented in this chapter reflect this fact.

Chicago will again be used as the area for application of the methodology. About eight percent of all trips in the six county Chicago SMSA and about 23 percent of all work-trips take place on transit. Most of the work-trips are to the CBD, where transit provides about 85 percent of CBD work-trips. The Chicago system is comprised of a variety of transit services which are both publicly and privately operated. These transit services are provided by 18 surburban bus companies, eight commuter railroads and the Chicago Transit Authority (CTA), which provides rail, rapid transit and bus service.

In the following section, relevant models used in this evaluation are described in some detail. For readers more interested in the policy applications of the methodology, this section may be skipped. An assessment of alternative transit policies is made, using these models, in the section on Mass Transit Strategies. Finally, in the summary section, the costs and emission reduction results are discussed.

MODAL CHOICE MODEL

The effectiveness and desirability of mass transit policies as environmental measures can be understood only through a fairly rigorous determination of the characteristics that determine travel behavior. Models designed to estimate these characteristics and to predict travel behavior have been in use for some years.[11, 15, 20] The approach that has yielded the best result is one that focuses on travel characteristics pertinent to individual decisions. The variables affecting a commuter's choice of travel mode which have been found to be important in making modal choices are (1) the income of the traveler, (2) relative travel time by travel mode, (3) relative money cost by mode, (4) trip purpose (work or nonwork) and (5) relative comfort and convenience.

These factors affect the choice of mode to different degrees under different conditions. The value of avoiding longer travel time increases with the income of the commuter, other things being equal, so that the sensitivity of the choice of travel mode to travel time differences is important in transportation decisions. In one important respect, mass transit has a substantial time disadvantage as compared with the automobile. This arises from the time required to get to and from mass transit stations, and from waiting time. During rush hour this time disadvantage is minimized by more frequent mass transit service and correspondingly reduced headway. Also, during this period the automobile is subject to greater congestion costs. For nonwork-trips, longer waiting times and lower parking costs are the important reasons that the automobile is used more frequently even for travel to the city center.

Differences in money costs and convenience of transportation modes also affect the mode choice. The impact of convenience relative to transportation costs also varies with the income of the traveler. Higher income groups place greater emphasis on differences in convenience than on differences in cost. Where community incomes increase over time such behavior works to the detriment of mass transit since the automobile generally has superior characteristics of flexibility and convenience. This explains in part the increased demand for auto trips over time.

These factors were considered in developing a modal choice model for Chicago.[27] In this model the dependent variable is the probability of choosing a specific mode of travel. This probability is a function of (1) alternative trip times between private automobiles and mass transit ΔT, (2) alternative trip costs ΔC, (3) income and (4) trip distance. Work- and nonwork-trips are analyzed separately. Distance of the trip to the CBD is used as a proxy for comfort. The expected relationships between the probability of a mode choice and these variables best conform to probit functions in which the dependent variable can be expressed as a probability. This type of function, having a characteristic "S" shape, is shown below.

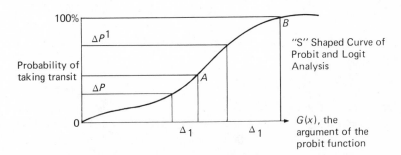

Figure 4-2. Probability of Choice Mode.

Mathematically the expression is

$$p = \int_{\infty}^{G(x)} \frac{1}{\sqrt{2\pi}} e^{-1/2\, t^2} dt \qquad (4\text{-}1)$$

for the probit function

where $G(x)$ is a linear function of the independent variables and p is the probability of the choices of modes.

$$G(x) = a + b\Delta c + c\Delta T + d \cdot \text{income} + e \cdot \text{distance} \qquad (4\text{-}2)$$

Data used in this model were based on a Chicago Area Transportation Study (CATS) 1956 home interior survey. This information was collected for the entire Chicago area and aggregated into zones. The equations estimated for $G(x)$ before adjustment for inflation, are shown below.

Work-Trip Equations

Car-rail choice: $G(x) = .76 - .0063\Delta C - .024\Delta T + 1.5 \times 10^{-5}$ income
$+ .0070$ distance $\qquad (4\text{-}3)$

Car-bus choice: $G(x) = -.89 - .0063\Delta C - .0083\Delta T + .083 \times 10^{-3}$ income
$+ .088$ distance $\qquad (4\text{-}4)$

Car or other choice: $G(x) = -.67 - .0068\Delta C - .012\Delta T + .051 \times 10^{-3}$ income
$+ .054$ distance $\qquad (4\text{-}5)$

Nonwork-Trip Equations

Car-rail choice: $G(x) = 1.6 - .011\Delta C - .020\Delta T + .23 \times 10^{-4}$ income
$+ .0052$ distance $\qquad (4\text{-}6)$

Car-bus choice: $G(x) = -.11 - .0091\Delta C - .0019\Delta T + .091 \times 10^{-3}$ income
$+ .077$ distance $\qquad (4\text{-}7)$

Car or other choice: $G(x) = .3 - .010\Delta C - .00058\Delta T + .66 \times 10^{-4}$ income
$+ .051$ distance $\qquad (4\text{-}8)$

A graphical representation of the effects of one of these factors, money cost differences, on the probability of mode choice is shown in Figure 4-3.
From these equations (after adjustments for changes in the value

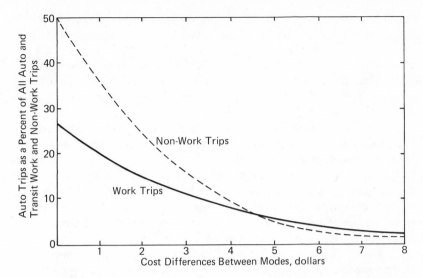

Figure 4-3. The Effect of Differences in Money Costs Between Modes on Auto Trips to the Chicago Loop.

of money) changes in travel mode and total automobile mileage were calculated for a variety of policy options. Because each policy generates a different estimate of automobile use in the CBD, the policies exhibit different air pollution effects.

There are several limitations related to data requirements that arise from the use of modal split models. Problems arise in connection with the accuracy of the basic data and from the way in which the model is used. The policies considered here involve changes in relative travel cost that are beyond the range of the data used to calibrate the model. Also, necessary aggregation of data may introduce inaccuracies. Finally, additional problems are created by the necessity of using CATS modal split survey data which may now be somewhat dated.

MASS TRANSIT COST MODEL

The modal split model calculates changes in mass transit ridership for the various policy options. The mass transit cost model transforms these ridership changes into the associated changes in costs for the mass transit system. This model, based on work by Hay et al [9], Morlok et al [18] and Hurter [12], takes as given the changes in bus and rail ridership predicted by the modal split model. The number of total CBD trips by all modes were assumed to be constant, as they are in the modal split model. The number of work-trips by mode was ob-

tained for each zone using the modal split model. These estimates by zone were
then superimposed on a Chicago Transit Authority map showing bus and train
routes. Work-trips were assigned to one of the 36 bus routes or one of the 12
train routes going to the CBD according to the following rules: Where one
bus or train station exists in a zone, the bus and train ridership respectively are
assigned to that station; where more than one station exists, ridership is split
equally between stations and assigned to the nearest station.

In this model only changes in peak ridership are translated into
costs. The assumption is that changes in nonpeak volumes do not add costs to
the system. Changes in peak ridership influence three important classes of cost
inputs—the number of vehicles, the number of vehicle miles and operator crew
days. Vehicle and crew costs represent the largest portion of potential cost
changes resulting from peak period operational changes. The inputs to the
model are transit headway, length of route, passenger traffic, wage rates and
vehicle costs on a route by route basis. The analysis assumes that route capacities are fixed—that is, trains, buses and labor assignments can be altered, but
laying more track is not considered. Travel on each of the major routes is
treated independently. Details of the cost calculation are found in Appendix B.

AUTOMOBILE TRAVEL COSTS

The changes in mass transit ridership affect not only mass transit costs but
also, as noted earlier, the costs of traveling on urban freeways and arterials.
Mass transit incentives which decrease the total traffic volume on roadways
lower the cost to drivers who continue to use the automobile by reducing automobile travel time and improving fuel economy. These travel time and cost
effects of changes in roadway volumes may be calculated using roadway speed-
volume relationships derived from empirical studies. The nature of the speed-
volume relationship for freeways is shown in Figure 4–4. As average freeway
volume per lane increases, speed falls until capacity is reached at around 2000
cars per lane per hour. This relationship shows travel time increasing with
volume until hypercongestion conditions occur. Hypercongestion is reached
at capacity when the relationship between flow and speed reverses and both
traffic flow and speed decrease. Under this condition the highway is saturated
and cannot accommodate more vehicles. This happens for freeways at speeds
of about 35 mph.

To calculate travel costs, the speed-volume curves are transformed
to a time-volume relationship which indicates the required minutes to travel
one mile on a roadway at a given volume. The amount of time spent in traveling
is multiplied by an estimate of the value of time to the commuter to obtain
a dollar cost, which is added to the other operating vehicle costs to determine
a total cost of travel by automobile on the roadway. This cost will increase with
the increased volume of vehicles which congest the road. This relationship can

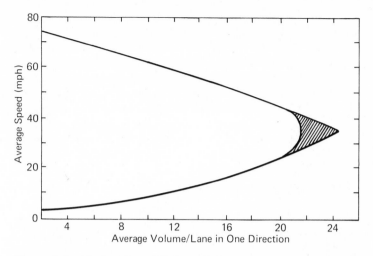

Figure 4-4. Typical Speed-Volume Relationship for Expressway.

be transformed into a price-volume curve where price is expressed in cents per vehicle mile of travel and volume in terms of vehicles per lane per hour.

There exist, in fact, two relevant price-volume curves, one representing the price perceived by the individual driver and another reflective of the costs paid by society as a whole. The private price-volume relationship is the average cost of travel per vehicle mile relevant for each roadway volume, while the social price-volume relationship is the additional total costs of travel from a unit increase in vehicle miles traveled. The social price reflects the change in total costs that occurs when a new car enters the system. This cost takes into account the effects of added congestion on all cars. The actual level of use of a road depends on the intersection of such price-volume curves with a roadway demand curve. Given a constant price of mass transit, the demand for roadway use declines with increasing roadway travel price. These relationships are given in Figure 4-5. In this figure AC (average costs) represents the costs per mile as perceived by the individual driver. The MC (marginal costs) curve represents the addition to total social costs from a unit increase in traffic flow. The demand curves D_1 and D_2 represent different levels of demand for use of the road such as might exist for different times of the day.

Since individuals make decisions based on privately perceived cost, the total vehicle miles generated will be where the demand curve crosses the average cost curve (point b for D_1) so that traffic flow is Q_1. Society is actually paying a price of travel per vehicle mile associated with the social cost curve (point c). For demand curve D_1, the difference in price between point b and point c is considered to measure the congestion costs associated with the last vehicle mile traveled. From a societal point of view, vehicle miles

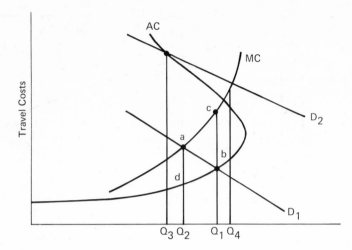

Figure 4-5. The Relationship Between Traffic Flow and the Costs of Congestion.

should be at Q_2 which is determined where the demand curve crosses the social cost curve (point *a*). The social cost of overusing the road in excess of private costs is given by area triangle *abc*.

In calculating the appropriate costs of congestion, we first determine the values of the divergence between private and social cost for different levels of traffic flow by comparing the average or private travel time costs with the total time costs imposed on others by a car entering the road system. This can be done from speed-volume relations discussed above. The source of data of speed-volume relationships on Chicago highways is a study performed by Keefer and sponsored by the Chicago Area Transportation Study.[4] Keefer performs a multiple correlation analysis using data from four types of roads: expressways, rural, urban with parking and urban without parking. Data were obtained by the "moving car" method where a driver takes an auto up and down a street and attempts to approximate the average speed of traffic.

Keefer's equations are of the form

$$S = a - bx \tag{4-9}$$

where:

s = the average speed,

x = the equivalent volume per 10 foot moving lane per hour, and

a and b = parameters determined by the regression equation.

Equivalent volume is equal to the product of actual volume and 1 plus the percentage of commercial vehicles. In actual volume a commercial vehicle was counted as the equivalent of two passenger cars.)

Using this relationship it is possible to calculate the difference in marginal social costs and private costs due to a change in highway flow. This can be found by determining the change in time costs that occurs for a unit change in traffic flow. For the Keefer relationships the divergence is of the form:

$$\Delta C = \frac{-c\,b\,x}{(a+bx)^2} \qquad\qquad (4\text{-}10)$$

where:

c = average cost per minute traveled per car, and

a, b, and x are defined as previously in 4–4.

In order to use this expression the value of time (c) must be determined. Guttman's theoretical and empirical work indicates that for rush hour travel in Chicago this is about $5 per hour and is above the after tax wage rate, presumably due to discomfiture of travelers during such hours.[7] These results do not appear unreasonable, but a conservative approach is adopted here by using approximately 75 percent of the after tax wage rate. The wage rate for automobile drivers in the Chicago area before taxes is estimated to be at least $3.33 per hour. This result is consistent with Ergun's estimate.[6] The computed value of travel time is then $2.50 per hour per person or about $3 per hour per vehicle with an average vehicle occupancy rate of 1.2 persons.

In addition to time costs, it is necessary to compute the direct operating and maintenance costs per vehicle. There is some evidence that operating costs are fairly constant between speeds of 35 and 55 mph where fuel mileage begins to drop.[2, 3] At lower speeds costs vary directly with speeds. We assume conservatively that costs are constant for Chicago expressways.

For arterials, lower speeds are common and it is necessary to take into account the fact that greater highway density imposes greater direct costs as well as greater time costs. Johnson [8] derives the following linear equation based on data from a Chicago Area Transportation Study report:

$$d = .829 + 0.312t \qquad\qquad (4\text{-}11)$$

where:

d = unit operating costs in cents per mile, and

t = unit time in minutes per mile.

The range of *t* is 1.71 to 5.45, or in terms of speed between 11 and 35 mph. If this is modified for inflation and changes in the price of gasoline we obtain:

$$d = 5.97 + 1.02t \tag{4-12}$$

This is consistent with Hewitt's calculations.[10]

On this basis, then, the social congestion costs in excess of private costs can be calculated for various traffic flows for Chicago's highways and arterials. These calculations for expressways and arterials, accounting for both vehicle and time costs in cents per mile, are given in Table 4-1.

MASS TRANSIT STRATEGIES

The strategies considered fall into four categories: (1) congestion tolls, (2) exclusive bus lanes, (3) parking strategies and (4) mass transit fare changes. For each of these strategies an attempt will be made to determine the environmental effects and the costs associated with implementation of the strategy. These results are used in determining the desirability and feasibility of the strategies in the same manner as in Chapters Two and Three.

Congestion and Environmental Tolls

Tolls for automobile driving would of course reduce the number of automobile miles driven. Some trips would be made by mass transit where previously they were by automobile, and some trips which previously were taken would not be. These effects would reduce automobile pollution and thus total pollution. There is, in fact, a strong rationale for automobile driving tolls on the basis of congestion alone. A substantial economic literature exists con-

Table 4-1.*   **Unaccounted-for Social Congestion Costs for Chicago Highways and Arterials**

Traffic Flow		
Vehicles per lane per hour	*Expressways (cents per mile)*	*Arterials (cents per mile)*
200	0.07	0.70
400	1.37	1.71
600	2.23	2.73
800	4.16	5.89
1000	4.44	10.44
1200	5.92	18.99
1400	9.55	37.09
1600	11.20	–

*For direct costs the relevant elasticity is the elasticity of operating costs with respect to traffic flow. This may be found by multiplying the elasticity of operating costs with respect to time by the elasticity of time with respect to flow.

cerning the misallocation of automobile trips on highways due to the underpricing of highway use.[23, 24, 28] The misallocation in question occurs because, as shown previously, users of highways do not consider the time cost they impose on others as congestion occurs. Thus, the real or social costs of highway use differ from the private costs.

The idea of a congestion toll is to levy a tax sufficient to eliminate the divergence between the private and social cost. The optimum traffic flow level occurs where additional private benefits as measured by a demand curve equal additional social costs as determined by the marginal social cost curve. The optimum tax would thus be one that equalled the divergence in marginal social and private costs at this point. Referring to Figure 4-4, the correct tax would equal the difference between points a and b, if D_1 were the relevant demand curve.

The ideal tax would be a fluctuating tax which varied as travel demand varies during the day. If such a tax were available as an efficient administrative device several beneficial results would follow. First, congestion would be lessened by a greater spreading out of peak traffic periods. There would be greater incentives to leave for work earlier or later reducing peak flow and thereby lowering peak emissions. Trucks, for whom congestion tolls would be up to three times as high as for cars because of their greater contribution to congestion, would travel more in off-peak hours. Nighttime truck deliveries, as shown in Chapter Three, have a substantial effect in reducing peak pollution levels. Second, congestion would be lessened by a greater use of mass transit, and this would also, of course, lower pollution levels. Third, a more efficient distribution among existing routes would occur.

The size of the appropriate congestion taxes for freeways and arterials can be read directly from Table 4-1. This table shows the excess of social costs of highway use over the privately perceived cost. The striking thing about these results is the high values of the taxes obtained. Even for rather low traffic volumes a tax is required. Traffic values on expressways and major arterials rarely fall below 400 cars per lane per hour. At this level of flow, a tax for congestion of about 1.7 cents per mile is required for arterials and 1.37 cents per mile for expressways. This tax only eliminates the social costs of congestion. To the tax must be added the additional social costs of pollution damages. The correct value would be less than one cent per mile as shown in Appendix A. For a 25 mile round trip a basic charge then would be between 63 cents and 75 cents. For rush hour trips, of course, appropriate tolls would be a good deal greater. A tax of not less than nine cents per mile is required for rush hour volumes of traffic exceeding 1,400 cars per lane per hour, on expressways. Two methods of applying such a tax are considered here.

Tolls as Rush Hour Licenses or as Metered Payments. This scheme involves use of the urban highway or arterials during specified (peak) periods of the day. This would not, of course, be an ideal tax once the fixed fee was paid, proper disincentives for use of the highways during periods of congestion would no longer be in existence. Nevertheless, some desirable diversion to less congested times and modes would occur. The problem of distinguishing between those who pay the fixed fee and those who do not might be solved by issuing license plates of different colors—e.g., red and blue. If a motorist wished to drive during rush hour, he would pay the extra fee and receive a set of red plates; those not paying the extra fee would receive blue ones. Anyone driving with blue plates during rush hours would be subject to a fine. The scheme contains a certain lack of precision in that people making short journeys on congested routes would be charged as much as those making longer journeys. Howerver, this approach would appear to be administratively feasible. The tax would be at least five cents and probably closer to ten cents per mile. The typical rush hour commuter drives 25 miles per day on expressways and works about 250 days per year. At five cents a mile, the fixed fee equivalent of the ideal tax then would be about $312 per year, and at ten cents a mile, $624 per year. Given the size of the requisite fee, it seems highly unlikely that this approach is politically feasible. In terms of pollution costs, of course, a fee which merely reduces social congestion costs to zero cannot be construed as a pollution control cost.

With regard to emission reductions consequences, a yearly rush hour license fee of around $300 diverts some automobile traffic from the CBD. Yet this diversion represents less than a five percent reduction in emissions of CO, HC and NO_x over and above the federal program effects. Since this program is essentially costless from a pollution control standpoint, the cost-effectiveness ratio is zero.

Gasoline Taxes as Motoring Tolls.   Gasoline taxes are also only an imperfect approximation to the correct set of taxes which should vary according to the level of congestion. A uniform gasoline tax may, however, be the best administratively feasible proxy available for the appropriate congestion tax. If a uniform gasoline tax is to be used the question is, What is the most appropriate single tax? The effects of four levels of uniform tax were evaluated using the modal split, congestion cost and emission models: these were a 5, 10, 15 and 20 cents per gallon tax added to existing gasoline prices.

Due to the congestion cost decreases, the net cost of these taxes to society was negative or zero. The pollution reductions were quite modest: 0.7, 4.0, 4.7 and 8.5 percent for carbon monoxide respectively. It is assumed that the revenue from such a tax is used to subsidize mass transit fare reductions. This constitutes a sizeable transfer of several million dollars a year from mostly middle and upper income groups, more likely to use automobiles, to lower income classes. Automobile users of course benefit from less congestion.

The appropriate gasoline tax from a congestion point of view is a weighted average of taxes at varying congestion levels. This tax is determined by calculating the relevant taxes at different times of the day weighted by volume of traffic during those periods. The appropriate formula is:

$$q = \sum_{i=1}^{n} \alpha_i q_i \qquad (4\text{-}14)$$

where:

q = weighted tax,

q_i = tax relevant to period i, and,

α_i = percent of total traffic in period i.

From empirical data relating time of day to variations in traffic flow and speed on roadways, it is possible to determine α_i, the percentage of average daily trips (*ADT*) according to hour of the day.

This procedure is applied to a typical Chicago freeway. The congestion tax, weighted to account for shifting diurnal demand, becomes 35 cents per gallon if 10 miles per gallon is assumed and 52 cents per gallon if 15 miles per gallon is assumed. Gasoline taxes over 20 cents per gallon were not considered politically feasible, and therefore emissions reductions were only considered for taxes less than 20 cents.

In terms of net congestion cost and emission benefits to society the essential problem with congestion tolls is that while society as a whole benefits in terms of congestion and pollution there is a considerable transfer of payments involved. This presents severe political problems for those tolls high enough to have any significant pollution reduction effects. Since the net cost to society is zero or negative, the cost-effectiveness ratio of gasoline taxes as pollution control measures turns out to be zero.

Parking Strategies

Strategies which change parking costs can influence driver behavior in the specific area in which a reduction in vehicle miles traveled is desired. By altering the cost of traveling to the CBD through parking surcharges, these strategies are primarily aimed at changing the travel decisions of commuters who work in the CBD and the travel mode and destination of shoppers who have

alternative shopping opportunities outside the CBD. In order to determine the
effect of parking taxes it is necessary to calculate (1) the effect of parking tax
increases on parking rates, (2) the extent to which parking rate increases raise
the costs of automobile commuters coming to the CBD and (3) the diversion
of parkers from the CBD in response to such cost increases. With respect to parking rate increases, the change in parking rates cannot be assumed to be the
amount of the parking tax since the tax may not be completely passed on to the
consumer. How much of the tax will be passed on in the form of parking price
increases will depend on demand and supply conditions for parking. In the case
of Chicago, the extent to which past parking taxes in Chicago increased rates
above the time trend indicates that parking prices may increase by about 60 percent of the added tax. This percentage can be used as the increase in automobile parking costs to the commuter.

Commuters have the option of responding to increased prices either
by parking farther away from the CBD in locations where rates are usually lower
or by switching to mass transit. For the first of these responses, automobile
users can lower the burden of the parking rate increase essentially by substituting time for money—that is, by parking farther away and walking to the CBD.
Ergun shows that nonwork-trips are affected relatively little by parking costs
in their parking location choice, presumably because of a lack of knowledge of
alternative opportunities and prices.[6] The situation with work-trips is quite
different since these parkers are quite senstitive to parking costs. Ergun's model
indicates that in response to uniform parking increases of between $1 and $4,
substantial parking would occur farther away from the CBD destination, so that
time is substituted for money costs.

In order to calculate the diversion of trips to mass transit, $1 and
$4 per day increases in parking rates were assumed and estimates of decreased
automobile trips made, based on the modal split model. By combining the diversion of parkers outside the CBD and the diversion of trips to mass transit,
the effectiveness of these parking surcharge strategies can be estimated. For the
$1 surcharge a reduction of less than four percent in CO, HC and NO_x is expect-
ed. For a $4 surcharge a reduction of almost 14 percent may be anticipated.
The $4 surcharge can be seen to have a significant impact on commuter trips,
which comprise about a quarter of the total vehicle miles in the CBD.

The extreme case of parking control is of course a complete ban on
parking in the CBD. The environmental effect of such a ban on private automobiles in the Chicago CBD would of course be considerable. With such a ban air
quality standards could be met. This would not, however, be the only benefit.
Recent unpublished work indicates that the excess road congestion costs for
central city traffic are very high indeed. Present speeds on CBD streets average
about nine miles per hour during the day. On many streets, however, and on
most streets during certain periods, average speeds are much less, amounting to
only a few miles per hour. Apparently figures as high as 50 cents per mile for

the excess congestion costs under present conditions may be appropriate. If private parking was banned, the benefits to passengers of remaining vehicles—taxis, buses, delivery trucks—would be substantial.

A ban on private cars in the CBD would, however, in the absence of alternative arrangements, materially affect the viability of the downtown area, and would not be tolerated by downtown merchants. The most logical alternative would be to provide both parking for all cars outside the CBD and substantial facilities in the form of buses and taxis for moving people between CBD stores and offices and the parking lots. To explore in detail the costs and benefits of this proposal is outside the scope of this book.

Changes in Mass Transit Fares

Changes in mass transit fares will also promote switching of ridership from automobiles to mass transit and will reduce both pollution and congestion. Substantial reductions in fares are necessary, however, to accomplish these results. Fare reductions, as opposed to the previously discussed methods of increasing costs to automobile users, have considerable political appeal. From the standpoint of the city government, lower cost trips enhance the viability of the CBD. In addition, mass transit is reportedly used disproportionately by the poorer city inhabitants so that fare reductions would constitute a greater benefit to the poor rather than the rich segments of the population.

Four fare policies are considered: (1) a 45 cent reduction (zero fare); (2) a 90 cent fare reduction and (3) fare increases of 25 cents and (4) 50 cents. It is desirable to establish the effects of fare increases as well as decreases, since increases on the order of magnitude of the above have been discussed as a means of increasing mass transit revenues. As with the other mass transit strategies, for each prospective fare change calculations are made for the CBD emissions effects, the change in costs to the mass transit system and the congestion savings or costs.

A 45 cent fare decrease. This policy reduces Chicago Transit Authority fares to zero. Train fares vary by the length of the trip but are above 45 cents even for short trips. The modal split model shows that this policy would reduce work-trips to the CBD by automobile by about 24 percent. Non-work-trips would be reduced by about 26 percent. This would have a small but significant effect on CBD emissions, reducing carbon monoxide by five percent. The costs of this reduction are slightly negative due to the congestion saving involved.

A 90 cent fare decrease. This policy involves a subsidy for all CTA riders and many commuter railroad riders. A reduction in CBD carbon monoxide emission of about eight percent would be produced. The reduction is thus about 30 percent greater than that from the 45 cent fare reduction. The loss of mass transit revenues, however, would be more than twice that of the 45 cent fare reduction due to the proportionately smaller number of commuters which would switch to mass transit in response to greater fare reductions. The net costs of this policy are negative because of the congestion savings but it seems likely that subsidy of mass transit on the scale required would be politically untenable.

Fare increases of 25 and 50 cents.   With continued inflation increased fares become more likely. A 25 cent and 50 cent fare increase would increase CBD carbon monoxide emissions by 1.9 percent and 4.4 percent respectively. The most important point for our purposes is that while fare increases of this magnitude would negatively affect emissions in the CBD, this effect would not be very great. The congestion costs in this case are positive but are not considered pollution control costs since fare increases are clearly not pollution reduction measures.

Exclusive Bus Lanes

A mass transit technique widely regarded as among the most promising is that of exclusive bus lanes.[1] Although mainly seen as a method of reducing travel time, the introduction of exclusive bus lanes would have emission effects as well. The increased use of buses could reduce automobile traffic and thus automobile emissions by a greater amount than the increase in emissions from the additional bus traffic. The technique is seen as relatively inexpensive since it generally utilizes existing fixed road capacity. The idea is that exclusive bus lanes would allow the high speed operation of a great number of buses operating with a short headway and that this would not only mean far lower travel times for those using the bus services, but lower travel times for remaining car drivers as well. Measurements of the effect on travel time must consider both bus and auto travel time changes, and these travel time effects are the crucial test of the desirability of this system. The creation of exclusive bus lanes, like those of the other mass transit strategies analyzed in terms of their emission reduction potential, was considered desirable only if it could be justified on congestion savings considerations alone.

A priori it is difficult to predict the travel time effects of exclusive bus lanes. Conversion of traffic lanes from automobile and truck use to bus lanes means of course that fewer lanes are available to automobile drivers. For situations in which lanes are removed from traffic going in the same direction as the buses, automobile traffic might move either more quickly or slowly, depending on how many passengers switched from automobile to bus. Ordinarily the amount of switching which would have to occur to speed up automotive traffic flow must be extremely large. The more usual procedure is to remove

---

1. The empirical data in this section for cities other than Chicago is taken from [20].

lanes from contraflow traffic—that is, lanes are removed from traffic flowing in the opposite direction to the bus lanes. Gain in travel time here depends in large part on the directional imbalance in traffic flow. Where this imbalance is large, the directional switching of lanes for bus use should produce travel time gains.

The analysis of data pertaining to exclusive bus lanes established near the Lincoln Tunnel on I-95, and on the Shirley Highway running between Springfield, Virginia and Washington, D.C. indicates that substantial patronage and time savings can occur from exclusive bus lanes where: (1) a lane is removed from contraflow traffic, (2) a new lane is built, (3) the exclusive lane alleviated an important bottleneck (4) a park and ride facility is provided or (5) sufficient patronage can be gained from those living and working within walking distance of the bus.

For other systems, data are available concerning changes in bus travel times before and after implementation of exclusive bus lanes. Data are also available concerning the direct implementation costs of these systems. These data are given for six systems in Table 4-2. The most striking thing about Table 4-2 is that for all systems the annual benefits exceed annual costs.

As far as environmental effects are concerned, however, it cannot be concluded that, even where favorable conditions exist, the exclusive lane will result in much lower vehicle emissions. A survey of new riders on an exclusive bus lane found that 21 percent had switched from car or car pools. The remaining 79 percent had switched from mass transportation.

In a limited way, Chicago has had exclusive or at least preferential bus lanes since 1956. These are preferential in the sense that a partially successful attempt is made to insure that these lanes are for exclusive bus use during selected periods. Altogether as many as 100 buses use the preferential facilities in the peak hours. These preferential lanes are confined primarily to the CBD. The question is whether or not Chicago could benefit from a more extensive use of exclusive or preferential bus lanes. In two main corridors of movement for Chicago P.M. peak motor vehicle movement has no strong directional flow. The assignment of an exclusive bus lane would then necessarily increase congestion from the remaining vehicles. Previous experience (e.g., Louisville) indicates that the savings in travel time by exclusive bus users would only marginally offset the loss in time by car users. In addition, lower speeds for automobiles significantly increase their operating costs as well as driver travel time and emissions.

Since Chicago has one of the best developed commuter rail systems in the nation and already has approximately 90 percent of its commuter travel to the CBD by mass transit, exclusive bus lanes might in some cases cause passengers to switch from rail to bus with no environmental gain or even a loss. Moreover, the switching from rail to bus on the basis of marginal time gains reduces the viability of the rail system. The net emissions effect might not be at

Table 4-2. Evaluation of Exclusive Bus Lanes

Location	Length of Exclusive Facility (miles)	Number of Passengers per Day	Aggregate Annual Savings—255 Work Days at $2.82 per Hour (1000s)	Annual Cost (1000s)	Annual Saving Minus Cost (1000s)
1. New Jersey	2.5	35,000	4,195	230*	3965
2. New York City–Long Island Expressway	2.0	7,500	1,798	132	1666
3. Boston–Southeast Expressway	8.4	2,500	412	142	270
4. Louisville	2.0	250	32	20**	12
5. San Juan	10.4 (one way)	NA	NA	NA	NA
6. Shirley Highway	9.0	16,500	3,362	840	2522

*The cost of capital is calculated at 10 percent per year.
**An estimate of cost data is incomplete for this system.

all positive. For the present, then, the argument for the use of exclusive lanes in Chicago as an environmental tool does not appear strong. This conclusion rests on the existence of a well-developed mass transit system, however, and may not be at all true for cities without viable mass transit alternatives.

COMPARISONS OF MASS TRANSIT STRATEGIES

All the policies that increase mass transit ridership have slightly negative costs due to the decrease in highway congestion costs associated with these policies. Thus, a discussion of the relative cost-effectiveness ratios such as concluded Chapters Two and Three is not appropriate. Because of the large number of policies considered, however, it is desirable to summarize some of the results in table form, and this is done in Table 4-3. One of the most striking results of the analysis was that, except for very large congestion or parking taxes, the emission reductions of any of the mass transit strategies appear to be modest. The most attractive mass transit policy from a political viewpoint is fare reductions, possibly coupled with a very modest increase in the gasoline tax. Reductions in fares, especially in off-peak fares, will help exploit economies of scale in mass transit and will be more politically acceptable than parking taxes or rush hour auto permits. Such fare reductions are economically feasible if supported by a gasoline tax, which would provide some subsidy to mass transit and a modest direct incentive switch from automobile to mass transit use. The viability of such a policy depends in part on the recognition of the congestion benefits accrued to those motorists continuing to use urban roads to travel to the CBD.

We have not examined the question of whether really fundamental changes in mass transit systems including large capital expenditures are desirable. There is no lack of critics who argue that increased investment in mass transportation and decreased investment in automobiles and highways represent the socially desirable choice. On the other hand many economists and transportation researchers point to the lack of financial viability of mass transit as evidence of its inefficiency as compared with the automobile. We do not examine these questions here in depth. However, some general points can be made.

The first point that needs to be made is that elimination of mass transit would have profound effects on the basic fabric of the Chicago land use pattern. Currently, at least 85 percent of work-trips to the CBD are by mass transit. It would be a physical impossibility for the CBD to handle the cars if they replaced mass transit. Really significant curtailment or elimination of mass transit would diminish enormously the importance of the CBD as a work center. This may or may not be desirable but the importance of the effect must be kept in mind. Four decks of parking over the entire CBD would be required to handle the cars required to supplant the mass transit system. The environmental effects would be profound.

Table 4-3.   Cost-Effectiveness of Mass Transit Policies

Strategy	Estimated Percentage Change CBD Air Quality, CO Only, for 1975 (PPM— eight hour average)	Strategy Cost. Present Value Cost for Six Year Program 1975–1980 (millions)
	(1971 base)	
A. Mass Transit Policies— Fare Changes		
1. 45¢ transit fare decrease	3.7%	−0.20
2. 90¢ transit fare decrease (subsidy)	5.5	−4.52
3. 25¢ transit fare increase	−1.8	3.15
4. 50¢ transit fare increase	−4.6	0.34
B. Parking Strategies		
1. $1.00 parking tax increase (8 hour rate)	3.7	−0.15
2. $4.00 parking tax increase (8 hour rate)	11.0	−4.17
3. Lots at end of transit lines	2.8	−3.20
4. Parking lots around Loop	5.5	NC[1]
C. Congestion taxes		
a. Rush hour licenses	3.2	−3.93
b. Gasoline taxes for SMSA*		
1. 5¢/gallon	1.0	NC[1]
2. 10¢/gallon	2.8	−0.49
3. 15¢/gallon	3.8	−1.03
4. 20¢/gallon	7.3	−1.75

*Assures all revenue collected over $100 million annually goes to reduce fares.
1. Not calculated.

The argument to greatly expand mass transit simply as an environ-mental measure seems a weak one. From Appendix C we find that a generous estimate of damages from light-duty gasoline vehicles in the Chicago SMSA is about $54 million per year. On a mileage basis this is less than one cent per mile. A pollution charge then would add at most about 25 cents to the daily commuting trip, and this would result in an insignificant switching from auto-mobiles to mass transit.

The expansion of mass transit in an effor to reduce congestion costs is a somewhat different matter; much higher subsidies are justifiable than for pollution. For rush hour periods charges as high as five to ten cents per mile may be used to subsidize transit. Taxes of this magnitude would increase mass transit ridership, and this increase in ridership would have beneficial environmental effects and would aid in meeting present operating mass transit deficits.

Thus, a reasonable argument can be made that mass transit should retain a place in the transportation network. Modest expansions of a mass transit system such as Chicago's may be justified on a cost-benefit basis; whether or not really substantial expansions are justified is problematical.

Chapter Five

Summary and Conclusions

The primary purpose of the preceding chapters has been to develop a methodology for analyzing significant issues presented by automobile pollution and to
determine the environmental effects of urban transportation policies. This
has been done by the development and application of a sequence of environmental, traffic, transportation and cost models to assess federal and local
control of transportation pollutants. The use of a behavioral model for determining the choice of travel and a congestion model for estimating highway congestion costs represents an innovative applications in an environmental context
and is therefore of particular interest. The results of applying this methodology
to Chicago indicate that the conclusions drawn and the methodology developed
have a wide applicability to large urban areas, and generate broader implications
for the way in which environmental policy is formulated. This chapter seeks
to summarize the policy and methodological implications of this effort and
attempts to assess their relevance to future environmental and transportation
planning.

NEW CAR STANDARDS

The major conclusion of this study with regard to new car standards is that
federal imposition of emission standards requiring elimination of 90 percent or
more of automobile emissions should be delayed until the 1980s. The case for
this conclusion consists of several parts but in sum is very persuasive. First, the
effects of the introduction of these standards would be small until well into the
1980s. The major impact of new car standards is felt several years after their
introduction as increasing percentages of cars in use become subject to the
standards. For this reason, emissions from automobiles have been declining for
some time and will continue to decline well into the 1980s whether or not
the standards requiring 90 percent or greater reductions are introduced. The

93

additional effects of these standards are marginal and at best their introduction would mean that a pollution reduction would be obtained about one year ahead of schedule. In addition, these standards would be of no help whatsoever in attaining the required 1975 air quality goals since they could only apply after that date.

Second, at least until the 1980s, 90 percent or greater emission reductions will probably require the use of the catalytic converter with its associated risks. Thus, the standards for the time being have greater risks associated with them than with previous standards because of the adverse secondary health effects of the converters. As the technological situation now stands, the attainment of these emissions standards requires that the adverse effects of the use of converters will be risked without a clear picture of the relative health impacts of the emission of sulfates and platinum associated with their use. The marginal reductions in regulated pollutants as a result of the use of the converters in the years immediately following their introduction must be balanced by the risk of creating a more severe problem in later years with respect to these previously unregulated pollutants. The lifetime reliability of the converters is also in doubt and may cause a significant increase in the cost of converter maintenance or replacement.

Third, given technology likely to be available in the 1970s, standards requiring removal of as much as 90 percent of automotive emissions are quite costly as compared with previous standards and considerably less cost-effective. Estimates of environmental damages which would be eliminated by these standards are a good deal less than the costs these standards impose. Moreover, the costs of these standards appear especially high, as we have seen, when compared with the costs of using local policies to reduce pollution in problem areas.

Ultimately, the value of standards requiring more than 90 percent removal of emissions must be measured in terms of what alternative methods of control will be available and what effect the growth in the use of automobiles will have on air quality in the next decade. These standards will be justified in the 1980s only if the costs and effects associated with the standards change substantially by that time. This may happen. Automobile emissions will probably begin increasing again in the mid-1980s, after a long decline beginning in the early 1970s, as the effects of existing standards become fully felt and the automobile population continues to increase. However, even when the effects of the 90 percent removal standards become fully felt the reduction in pollution levels from what they would otherwise be is only about an additional 12 percent of CO and HC, although 60 percent for NO_x. How important it will be to obtain this reduction at that time may depend on how rapidly the automobile stock is increasing by the mid-1980s, but it is very difficult to make predictions that far in advance.

The cost of meeting these more stringent standards will of course be less in the 1980s if new engine technology becomes available. One procedure might be to make a judgment of the value of meeting these standards by some date in the 1980s and to use this value as a tax that must be paid by the automobile manufacturers for nonperformance. Such a procedure seems economically appropriate. If the cost of meeting these standards is less than the tax the technology will be forthcoming. If the costs are greater it is not desirable to adopt the technology. Better yet, the tax could vary according to the date by which the standards were met so that the timetable itself would be the variable subject to the economic incentive. This would be a more appropriate and flexible procedure than using a fixed date to determine an all-or-nothing decision based on a presently uncertain technology.

TWO CAR STANDARDS

A second significant point with respect to new car standards relates to their geographical uniformity. An important conclusion of this study is that a two car emission standard would produce substantial savings with only negligible adverse effects. The rationale for the two car standard lies in the fact that nonurban damages from automobile pollutants are much less than in urban areas, and that such a system would not only be less expensive, but would be more equitable. The view has been expressed that federal new car standards reflect the wishes of the upper and upper middle income classes, expecially those segments living in metropolitan areas.[1] A two car standard would be more equitable not only on a geographic basis but on an income basis, since incomes are lower in rural areas. A two car standard based on division of cars registered in SMSA and non-SMSA counties or by states would produce a workable system without great enforcement difficulties and the adverse effects on air quality in areas of high pollution from the operation of lower standard cars would be quite small.

A variety of possible combinations of standards could be adopted. The one suggested here would require about 83 percent control of HC and CO and 32 percent control for NO_x for SMSA counties, and the 1970 standards for non-SMSA counties. This would result in yearly savings on a national basis of about half a billion dollars a year compared with a uniform system meeting the 1975 interim standards and a savings of over two billion dollars a year on a national scale compared with a uniform system attaining about 93 percent emission control.

A type of two car standard is involved in using a policy of selective retrofit of vehicles. Retrofit allows the implementation of more severe standards to deal with problem areas. Such a policy may be particularly attractive if federal emission standards are generally relaxed. It was found that four retrofit devices appear potentially attractive and warrant further investigation. These were (1) speed control exhaust, (2) American Pollution Control System, (3) spark retard and (4) simple exhaust recycle. The catalytic muffler is also attractive assuming the adverse secondary health defects turn out to be manageable.

LOCAL STRATEGIES

One of the most important findings of this study is that local strategies represent superior alternatives to the new car programs as a means of reducing emissions in central cities. This finding is part of a more fundamental observation and a more fundamental criticism of the federal approach to the effect that selective strategies dominate uniform ones in cost-effectiveness. The suggestion that two (or more) car standards are appropriate and desirable in federal policies also exemplifies the general observation that selective policies usually dominate uniform ones.

     A more narrow policy implication of the same type is that the present timetable for meeting air quality standards could best be met, not by an extension of national uniform emission standards, but by the implementation of local controls. If the need for emission reductions stems from the requirement to eliminate air quality violations in central cities by the mid-1970s, then the substitution of localized controls would seem to be a most cost-effective approach, especially considering the uncertain consequences of the introduction of catalytic converter technology. Substitution of local programs should allow sufficient time (given suitable tax or regulatory incentives) to develop and implement superior automotive reduction mechanisms. Estimates are that the early 1980s represent a reasonable target date for full real implementation of available new technology.

     Of course, the choice of specific local control strategies depends on the local traffic and transportation conditions. The cost-effectiveness calculations applied in Chicago showed such strong patterns that it is quite probable that similar conclusions will be reached regarding the relative effectiveness of these strategies in other cities.

Traffic Flow Strategies

     What local strategies are desirable depend on the goals to be reached. Where the goal is to reduce levels of CO over a short time horizon, strategies aimed at increasing traffic flow show a definite superiority. Due to the decrease in congestion the costs of the strategy are negative, and even if the congestion effect is ignored the costs are small. However, increases in traffic flow, while they decrease emissions of CO and HC, increase emissions of NO_x. Inclusion of the effect of NO_x emissions produces a deterioration in cost-effectiveness by a factor of three.

     For a time period of more than one year, traffic flow strategies may lose effectiveness as new cars are attracted into the area by the increased speed. Elimination of on-street parking is less suspect in terms of attracting new vehicles into the CBD as the attractiveness of increased traffic flow is offset by the net fall in parking spaces. Thus, the combination of computerized traffic flow with reductions in the number of parking spaces through elimination of spaces or parking taxes might have longer term effects of a reasonable duration. Nevertheless, in view of present enforcement practices with regard to the effects of on-street parking in the CBD, considerable suspicion is justified with regard to the effects of on-street parking bans. Even small enforcement failures would have important speed and emission effects, since it only takes one car parking on a street in violation of the ban to reduce effective road width and thereby reduce speed and increase emissions.

Selected Central City Vehicles

Among the most promising local strategies are those aimed at vehicles which make a disproportionate contribution to the pollution of problem areas, usually the central business district. Taxi and truck strategies are the best of this type.

Taxi strategies which involve retrofit with catalytic converters or conversion of taxis to liquid petroleum gas (LPG) are among the most attractive both on cost-effectiveness grounds and on grounds of feasibility. The effects of retrofit or conversion are fairly substantial and the costs are quite reasonable. Indeed, the costs given are probably high. The retrofit policy is more attractive than conversion in that it does not raise questions of the availability of fuel and interfaces well with the present plan for equipping post–1974 vehicles with catalytic converters. However, again, the mufflers suffer a disadvantage of unknown magnitude in that they produce small platinum and palladium particles and sulfuric acid.

Little attention has been given to strategies focused on the large truck population in general, yet strategies focused on trucks in central business districts appear attractive. An important advantage of the truck strategies is that they produce a sizable effect. Truck strategies involve conversion of trucks operating in the CBD to LPG or the partial rescheduling of truck delivery hours. Retrofitting of trucks appears too expensive at this time given unresolved engineering problems. Fuel conversion is especially attractive on a cost basis and, indeed, this policy may have negative costs aside from administrative costs. Consideration, of course, must be given to questions of the availability of fuels.

Rescheduling of truck delivery hours so that half of the deliveries occur after the evening rush hour is the only policy that involves a spreading out rather than a reduction of emissions. It is also one that is particularly effective in terms of reducing violations. One important uncertainty involves the opposition of the merchants and other goods receivers in view of the fact that they bear most of the costs. It is clear, however, that the truck strategies warrant careful attention, given the increasing importance of CBD trucks to emissions and the fact of the declining contribution of automobiles to CBD emissions.

Emission-related Maintenance for Existing Vehicles

An understanding of inspection systems is particularly important given its popularity among federal, state and local officials. Many localities have inspection-maintenance systems either in operation or scheduled.

The various inspection-maintenance strategies produce quite different and interesting results. The cost-effectiveness appears quite sensitive to the testing procedure adopted. For the Idle Mode emission test adopted by Chicago and other localities, the inspection-maintenance strategy is not as cost-effective as other strategies focused more closely on vehicles operating just in the central business district. Although this strategy produces a sizable effect, extensions of this inspection system to larger geographical areas are increasingly and strikingly less cost-effective.

However, inspection-maintenance systems based on certain other testing procedures appear to produce more favorable cost-effectiveness performance. The best results appear to be attained when tests of moderate complexity such as the Key Mode are used. The crucial variable in determining the relative costs of these testing regimes is the respective gasoline savings associated with maintenance necessary to pass the emission test. Although any effective testing system will produce gasoline savings, the amount varies in effectiveness in reducing emission of CO and especially HC. The cost saving figures associated with the gasoline savings must be regarded as tentative, but there is little question that the Key Mode is cheaper than the Idle Mode from a social point of view in spite of its greater equipment costs. The difference in gasoline savings for the two modes justifies this conclusion, even for the comparisons least favorable to the Key Mode.

A final but important qualification for this strategy lies in the possible levels of correlation between test results and emission reductions. No testing region is perfect and a variety of techniques can be used to pass the tests without reducing emissions, though this is truer of Idle Mode than of Key Mode tests. Thus, the question of the quality controls associated with the maintenance work is an important one.

Most jurisdictions have adopted the Idle Mode test and the question arises, Why has this test been adopted when it is not the one most cost-effective? The hypothesis susggested here is that jurisdictions are attracted to the Idle Mode test because their own costs are lower and because of lack of knowledge concerning the gasoline savings from the tests.

In considering the cost-effectiveness of the local emission pollution control policies discussed, care must be taken to define precisely what the objectives of the program are and should be. For local control programs, if the objective is to meet air quality standards as a stop-gap measure, the choice of policy will tend to favor those measures which have a small investment and which affect only those vehicles operating in highly polluted areas and those pollutants in excess of the standards. In general, those policies which are restricted in the same manner as the goals they are intended to reach are most cost-effective. Where, as in the present case, the local goal is to reduce extreme CO readings for a small geographical area, policies aimed quite specifically at this goal are apt to be superior to more general strategies which achieve the same result. Though this is an obvious point, it is not one that policymakers seem always to have been absolutely aware of.

Mass Transit

Insofar as mass transit can reasonably replace the automobile it has enormous potential to reduce transportation emissions and, incidentally, to reduce highway congestion. The key to appreciating what uses can and cannot be made of mass transit as an environmental tool is an understanding of the relationship between mass transit and urban form and, indeed, urban politics.

The importance of understanding these relationships is shown by the counterintuitive result that complete elimination of mass transit is in fact a method of reducing rather than increasing pollution concentrations. How is this? The answer is that well-developed central business districts rely on mass transit systems for their existence. Only where mass transit is able to feed large numbers of workers and shoppers towards a central point can a really well-developed downtown such as New York's or Chicago's exist. Without the concentration of vehicles and population associated with downtown areas, the most important problem area associated with transportation pollution would disappear.

Of course, it is possible to use mass transit as a substitute for automobile trips other than those going to downtown areas. A mass transit system could be developed focused not on downtown trips but on those normally made by automobile to other than downtown areas. The problem here is that at present this is not a very feasible strategy due to the superiority in comfort and time flexibility of the automobile. Considerable subsidies would have to be given directly to mass transit riders to induce adequate ridership.

Given the existence of downtowns and downtown-oriented mass transit, the more realistic policy consideration is, what is the best use that can be made of mass transit as an environmental tool? In order to evaluate this question and other mass transit policy questions an application was made of transportation behavioral models in an environmental context. These models when combined with the technical models were sufficient for a rather complete evaluation of costs and effects associated with a wide range of mass transit policies. The modal split model provided estimates of the change in ridership by modes in response to policies affecting the costs and time of travel. The congestion model allowed the inclusion of the often ignored congestion costs or savings associated with different mixes of automobile and mass transit vehicle populations. The use of these models is an important addition to the environmental evaluation of mass transit cost calculation since the congestion costs can be a dominant consideration.

Other acceptable mass transit policies appear to have definite, though limited, effects on central city pollution levels. Of the additional strategies examined fare reductions possibly coupled with gasoline taxes seem a more attractive as well as a more politic method of attracting ridership than other methods. Other mass transit strategies seem unlikely to be adopted on political grounds. One would expect considerable opposition to substantial downtown parking taxes from downtown merchants. Rush hour licenses, while attractive on a cost-effectiveness basis, are excluded on political grounds since appropriate license fees should run over $300 per car per year to have any sizable effect. Exclusive bus lanes show some promise, but only in particular cases, and in any event their overall environmental effect would be very small. Thus, under the assumption made in the analysis, mass transit strategies are unlikely to be significant as a short-run pollution plan. The basic attractiveness of these policies in terms of their cost-effectiveness ratios was derived from the saving in congestion time costs of drivers in relation to increased mass transit costs rather than from pollution benefits. The significance of this finding relates not only to environmental policy but also to the present debate regarding the subsidization of mass transit. Increased expenditures or subsidy of mass transit must therefore be derived from other considerations than the external pollution benefits of increasing mass transit ridership.

Another interesting and potentially attractive proposal is, in essence, to ring the Loop with parking from which really good public transportation would operate. This would reduce central city congestion, which is very expensive in the time costs it imposes. Remaining vehicles operating on city streets would be essentially taxis, buses and delivery trucks. Such a strategy would work well if taxis were freely licensed so as to expand service and reduce fares, and if bus and jitney service were expanded for the downtown area. Such a policy is probably politically workable since, if anything, it would improve the downtown areas as a shopping market. This strategy would in effect eliminate most cars from the Loop and would thus have a significant impact on Loop emissions. To a certain extent the reduction in automobile emissions would be offset by increases in bus and taxi emissions. Per passenger, however, bus emissions are much less than automobile emissions. Taxis, as has been pointed out, constitute an easily identifiable fleet that may be singled out at little cost for selective emission reduction either by retrofit or conversion to gaseous fuels. Thus, in sum, the policy of forcing automobiles to park outside the central business district, and providing mass transit for trips within this district and be-

tween the district and the parking lots, is one which promises substantial
environmental improvements and which at the same time has a potential for
being both feasible and socially inexpensive.

In considering the mass transit results of Chpater Four one should
keep in mind that the environmental effects alone produce a fairly weak justification for the various policies. Not only do the environmental benefits from
reducing automobile travel work out to no more than a penny per mile, but
the justifiable investment in mass transit is limited by the opportunity cost of
not adopting other low cost pollution control alternatives. Comparable or
greater reductions can be achieved by taxi or truck fuel conversion for under
$200,000 per year. This represents an almost imperceptible level of subsidy to
mass transit if the viewpoint were taken that mass transit was saving society the
cost of these pollution control measures and should therefore receive this amount
as subsidy. It works out to much less than one cent per passenger trip as a form
of subsidy in the Chicago case. This is not intended to mean that mass transit
should not be subsidized but rather that justification for subsidization cannot
properly be made on pollution grounds alone.

In the case of the extension of a system or the creation of a new
mass transit system, the creation of mass transit travel opportunities may generate different land use patterns in the city and reduce the long-run growth in the
use of the automobile. Certainly areas such as the CBD in Chicago or New York
could not have been developed without an extensive mass transit system. By
changing the basic configuration of origins and destinations in an urban region
over several decades, as well as by altering mode choice decisions, mass transit
as a pollution control tool cannot be directly compared to other localized pollution control strategies.

INTERDISCIPLINARY METHODOLOGY

One of the most important contributions of this work lies in its methodology.
The significance and accuracy of the conclusions depend substantially on the
value of the methodology used. The methodology used here is felt to be appropriate and useful over a broad range of environmental problems related to transportation. The development and application of a sequence of environmental,
transportation and economic models was shown to be necessary in order to
accurately identify the impact and costs of federal and local pollution control
programs. Because the basic emission and cost calculations associated with a
given policy may involve such factors as the future age distribution of cars, the
operating conditions of automobiles in the area, and the speed of traffic flow,
the evaluation of environmental policies requires the development of a rather
wide array of models. In this study an emission factor model, a regional transportation model, an automobile registration model, a highway congestion model
and a number of economic models were all required.

To review briefly the general procedure employed in applying the models, first an emission factor model was utilized to determine the emission rates of vehicles for different years. This model utilized data concerning deterioration rates of emission over time, cold start effects, the emission characteristics of each of several vehicle classes and the effect of pollution control devices and fuel options. The emission factor model was linked where appropriate with a registration model which predicted over time the number and age distribution of automobiles. This latter model is sensitive to factors changing the relative prices of new and used automobiles such as new car safety features or cost-increasing pollution control devices. This model was combined with the output of a regional transportation model simulating automobile trips. The combination of these models generated a pollution profile of the region.

In the case of mass transit policies, a modal split model was needed to indicate the alteration in the vehicle mile projections due to the effect of the transit incentives. This model predicts the mode used for rides to the central business district on the basis of price, time, income and comfort variables. This basic model allows the determination of effects for a variety of mass transit policies. A traffic flow or congestion model was also needed to adjust the prediction of vehicular speeds on roadways due to the shifting of a percentage of the vehicle trips to mass transit. This congestion model utilized studies of the relationship between traffic flow and traffic speed. These were converted into a travel time-traffic flow relationship which, using appropriate estimates of the value of time and the relationship between speed and vehicle operating cost, were in turn converted into a model establishing the relationship between traffic flow and travel cost.

A cost model, analogous to the emissions model, was then used to assess the costs of the automobile and mass transit policies considered. This model converted capital, operating and maintenance costs to an equivalent present value basis. The model is sensitive to the age distribution of vehicles and incorporates a learning curve concept by which the costs of a particular control technology fall over time as experience with manufacturer and installation associated with the technology reduces its costs.

The cost calculations applied to mass transit were somewhat more complex. Here it was necessary to determine the costs imposed on the mass transit system by ridership changes and the congestion costs or savings of changes in automobile trips. Congestion cost estimates were developed through analysis of speed-volume relationships coupled with estimates of the value of time and the effect of speed on operating costs.

Finally, estimates of environmental damage from transportation pollutants were generated. However, relative changes among the transportation pollutants were generated. Relative changes among the transportation pollutants can be determined, and these weights applied to reductions in pollutants to generate a single measure of effectiveness. These models are used in conjunction with appropriate empirical data to produce estimates of the costs and effects of realistic policies for a typical urban area.

PRINCIPLES OF POLICY FORMATION

This methodology concerning envirnomental transportation problems has been presented and illustrated through concrete application to a real situation. However, this approach yields more than a ranking of specific strategies. Implicitly, it also yields insight into the broadest aspects of policy formation itself. The methodology provided here shows that cost-effectiveness analysis can be applied to important environmental problems associated with transportation. Specifically, we have shown that cost-effectiveness analysis can be used to evaluate the federal program for reduction of transportation pollutants. The application of cost-effectiveness analysis to the evaluation of federal policies, and to alternative policies, allows a meaningful ranking of the policies in terms of attractiveness.

One of the more important principles of policy making to emerge from this study is that care should be taken to define the problem and to match this carefully defined problem with an appropriate solution. This has not been done by the federal program and this failure is most clearly reflected in the uniformity of emission regulations. Pollution problems associated with the automobile vary considerably from area to area; the nature of the solutions should also vary. In particular, striking examples of this principle are found in the two car strategies, as mentioned above, and selective retrofit strategies, and the significant contribution that can be made by purely local strategies such as traffic flow, selected vehicle programs or mass transit strategies. These strategies reduce pollution in problem areas for costs that are a fraction of those encountered in the uniform program.

Apparently, cost-effectiveness analysis can make significant contributions to the evaluation of environmental transportation policies. The use of this technique becomes especially important in cases, the most common sort of cases, in which pressure or interest groups may secure regulations or laws favorable to their interests but not to the broadly defined social interest. When cost-effectiveness analysis is well used it makes the choice of socially inferior policies more conspicuous and therefore more difficult. Cost-benefit analysis is of even greater help in this regard since it not only provides a ranking of the policies, but also makes some contribution toward determining who are the gainers and the losers and whether or not the total gains from the policy exceed the total losses.

A second principle of policy formation relates to the way in which the timing of the policy enters the calculations of cost and effectiveness. The most notable example of this relates to the timing of the emission and air quality standards. The primary air quality standards must be met by 1975. In the case analyzed here, however, delay by one or two years of the date for meeting these standards would allow these to be met through the effects of new car standards without any supplemental strategies, given the original emission timetable.

The importance of the delay factor in the effectiveness of new car emission standards on air quality is significant in a second way. Catalytic converters may produce harmful effects by the emission of unregulated, but potentially more toxic, pollutants. Thus, policy decisions regarding the use of such devices should be made after the determination of such dangers, especially since the harmful effects may not be felt for several years after introduction of such a device.

A third implication regarding environmental policy development can be derived directly from the nature of the required methodology. In order to evaluate any of the control measures, it was necessary to link together a series of models each of which in some way depended on statistical data and procedures. The results of this evaluation in terms of emission reduction must then be considered as statistical in nature. The method by which such emission reduction estimates are compared with the required emission reductions tends to blur the statistical nature of environmental policy analysis by using a single air quality observation upon which to base required reductions. The weakness of this approach was illustrated in the Chicago situation. In Chicago, the use of the 1973 air quality data rather than the 1971 data results in a 20 percent increase in the reduction required to meet the air quality goals even though the air quality data clearly show that air quality has been improving. This situation results from the use of the second highest air quality reading to define air quality and to determine the reduction in emissions which is required. The point is that air quality is also primarily a statistically defined phenomenon based on the whole distribution of readings and that decision based upon a single extreme observation would be inappropriate.

In short, we find that a more explicit identification of costs and effects must be made in formulating environmental transportation policy. More attention must be given to the basic structure which must always lie behind good policy decisions. The magnitude, the timing, the procedures for calculation, the coverage and the flexibility of the air quality and emission standards all retain important deficiencies. If important deficiencies are found in the federal emission and air quality standards, by implication they must also exist in the policy structure that has produced these standards. The application of such cost-effectiveness techniques as shown in this book can significantly improve future policies.

Appendix A

Damages from Transportation Pollutants

R.O. Zerbe

Knowledge concerning air damage from automobile emissions is necessary in order to calculate the effectiveness of transportation strategies. Ideally one would like to know the damage produced at each level of emission. This, however, involves knowing (1) the relationship between emissions and air quality and (2) the relationship between air quality and damages. Such knowledge would allow a cost-benefit analysis rather than simply cost-effectiveness calculations. Unfortunately, knowledge that would allow such calculations is limited. Some rough calculations can, however, be made. What can be done with considerably more accuracy is to provide relative damage weights of the transportation pollutants. This will allow a braoder based calculation of cost-effectiveness for the various strategies. This is done in the following section.

RELATIVE DAMAGE WEIGHTS

Two sources of data exist for calculating relative damage weights (or severity factors) for the various pollutants. Babcock has developed an index to allow an equivalent measurement of pollution (Pindex), and this involves calculation of severity factors.[1] These severity factors are based on air quality standards. The latest version of this, published by Babcock and Nagda, is thus one useful source of severity factors.[2]

In addition, substantial work in developing pollution damage weights has been done by Oak Ridge in developing the Oak Ridge Air Quality Index (ORAQI).[3] This index accounts for nonlinearity in pollution damage and is based on work indicating that damages increase more rapidly than pollutant levels for concentrations greater than the federal standards. Thus, ORAQI does not contain a single set of severity factors or tolerance factors as does Pindex; the severity factors per unit of pollution would depend on the particular air quality. For Chicago's air quality, ORAQI levels can be calculated and the implied severity factors derived. The severity factors derived from Pindex and ORAQI can be seen in Table A-1. No weight is given by ORAQI for hydrocarbons directly; the contribution of reactive hydrocarbons is accounted for by the oxidants. The weight used by ORAQI for particulate matter (PM) is measured in different units for the other pollutants.

The factors derived from Pindex for PM are more appropriate. For ORAQI, the weight for PM is suspiciously low and the absence of a weighting factor for hydrocarbons renders it less useful. However, the concept of nonlinearity of damages implicit in ORAQI is preferable. A composite set of severity factors for Chicago is therefore derived by using the factors from Pindex for PM and HC and using the ORAQI-derived factors for the other pollutants. Generally, cost-effectiveness calculations in the body of the paper use the Pindex weights, although the composite weights and those used by Steinbruner and Jacoby are sometimes used to determine the effect of varying the weights.

DAMAGES FROM AUTOMOBILE POLLUTION

Automobile emissions represent a very large percent of total emissions of air pollutants if measured by weight or volume. This is illustrated in Table A-2 which shows that transportation accounts for 60 percent by weight of all pollution. The bulk of this comes from the gasoline automobile. Most of this pollution is thus emitted at ground level in close proximity to population centers. It is on this basis that the automobile is usually referred to as the most important pollution source.

Babcock and Nagda's severity factors applied to contributions by source show that, nationally, transportation accounts for 14.7 percent of pollution by damage, and that gasoline automobiles account for 11.1 percent. These figures are, of course, in contrast to the figures showing transportation accounting for 60 percent of pollution. These new figures suffer from two defects: they do not take into account the technical conditions under which the emissions occur, such as height of emission source and meteorological

Table A-1. Relative Harm per Unit of Pollution

	PM	*SO$_x$*	*NO$_x$*	*CO*	*Oxidants*	*HC*
Babcock-Nagda (Pindex)	2.20	1.24	1.00	.042	5.59	.419
ORAQI (Chicago)	.007	3.86	1.00	.055	14.00	–
Composite index	2.20	3.86	1.00	.055	–	.419
Total	–	–	1.00	.750	–	1.00

Table A-2.   Emissions by Source (in millions of tons)

	CO	SO_x	HC	NO_x	PM	Miscellaneous	Total*	Percent
Transportation	66	1	12	6	1	1	86.0	60.0
Industry	2	9	4	2	6	2	25.0	17.4
Power Plants	1	12	1	3	3	–	20.0	13.9
Space Heating	2	3	1	1	1	–	8.0	5.6
Refuse Disposal	1	1	–	–	1	1	4.0	3.1
Totals*	72	25	18	12	12	4	143.0	100.0

*May not add to totals because of rounding.

Table A–3. Percentage Distribution of Air Pollution Source by Damage Weight (Pindex)

	Estimate One	Estimate Two
Transportation	15.7	19.6
External Combustion	52.8	40.8
Industrial Process	23.2	29.0
Solid Waste	4.8	6.0
Miscellaneous	3.3	4.1
Total	100.0	100.0

condition; and they do not take into account differences in the extent of exposure of people and materials to the emissions. Automobiles produce most of their emissions in cities at ground levels, where exposure of people and materials to emissions is greater than for most other sources. For our purposes there is a third defect in that the figures are for the nation, not for the Chicago area. This latter defect, however, can be remedied.

Calculations from unpublished data for Chicago showing the percentages of contributions by source to damages as damage contribution can be calculated by weighting with severity factors obtained as the reciprocal of the Babcock-Nagda tolerance factors: Babcock indicates that Chicago would be perhaps the most typical city in terms of application of the severity factors, and these considerations of nonlinearity of pollution damage would be less important. The calculations for Chicago are shown in Table A–3.

Two estimates are given, since there are substantial grounds for suspicion that there is an error resulting in a substantial overestimate in the tons of pollution produced by one of the sources contributing to the external combustion category. Estimate One may overstate the contributions of this categroy and thus understate the relative contributions of the other categories. Estimate Two is obtained by eliminating all contributions from the suspect industry. The correct estimates must then lie between Estimates One and Two, and the damage contribution of transportation must lie between 15.7 and 19.6 percent. In the absence of further data, the best estimate of the true value will be the mean of the above two estimates, or 17.7 percent. The figures for Chicago are fairly typical of many urban areas, and thus the estimate used here had a rough applicability to many cities. The various transportation contributors to damages, adjusted to yield a total of 17.7 percent of total urban damages, are shown in Table A–4.

Another estimate can be made by adjusting the Chicago emission figures by the composite severity factors mainly consisting of factors derived from ORAQI as developed in Table A–5. This table shows the percentage damage contributions for transportation sources in Chicago after adjusting and normalizing yields.

Table A-4. Contribution of Transportation Components to Air Pollution Damage (Pindex)

Source	PM	SO$_x$	NO$_x$	CO	HC	Total*	Percent of Total
Light duty gasoline	0.6	0.2	3.3	1.8	6.5	12.3	69.5
Heavy duty gasoline	0.0	0.0	0.6	0.2	1.1	1.9	10.7
Off-highway gasoline	0.0	0.0	0.1	0.1	0.2	0.3	1.7
Diesel, on highway	0.1	0.1	0.9	0.0	0.1	1.1	6.2
Diesel, off highway	0.0	0.0	0.1	0.0	0.0	0.1	0.6
Diesel train	0.1	0.2	0.2	0.0	0.1	0.7	4.0
Airplanes	0.1	0.1	0.1	0.0	0.1	0.5	2.8
Vessels	–	–	–	–	–	0.1	0.7
Gasoline handling evaporation loss	0.0	0.0	0.0	0.0	0.7	0.7	0.7
Total	0.9	0.6	5.3	2.1	8.8	17.7	100.0

*Figures may not add to totals because of rounding and because figures less than 0.1 are not reported but may enter totals.

It is now possible to make a rough calculation of pollution damages from transportation. Barret and Waddell, in summarizing the existing literature on air pollution damage, arrive at a figure of about $16 billion for the country for 1971. Babcock and Nagda, in adjusting this figure for omissions for CO effects and certain HC and NO$_x$ property and health-related effects, arrive at a figure of $20 billion. The health damages added by Babcock-Nagda are appropriate additions. The methods used to estimate the property damage, however, make it likely that the effects of the omitted pollutants were in fact picked up by measurements on the included pollutants, due to the high correlation of omitted and included pollutants. Adding only the additional health effects,

Table A-5. Contribution to Damages by Air Pollution Source adjusted by composite index (ORAQI)

Source	Chicago: Percentage Contribution
External combustion	67
Internal combustion	0
Industrial processes	20
Solid waste incineration	3
Transportation	8
Miscellaneous	2

**Table A-6.   Contribution to Damages by Transportation
Components percentage contribution (ORAQI)**

Source	PM	SO_x	NO_x	CO	HC	Total
Light-duty gasoline vehicles	0.303	0.319	1.97	0.652	1.87	5.12
Heavy-duty gasoline vehicles	0.023	0.024	0.34	0.178	0.317	0.89
Light-duty gas, off-highway	0.005	0.005	0.048	0.046	0.064	0.168
Heavy-duty diesel	0.042	0.146	0.536	0.017	0.022	0.763
Diesel, off highway	0.006	0.021	0.074	0.002	0.003	0.106
Diesel, rail	0.008	0.400	0.120	0.006	0.033	0.647
Air, military	0.006	0.002	0.001	0.000	0.003	0.013
Air, civil	0.003	0.001	0.001	0.002	0.003	0.009
Air, commercial	0.100	0.038	0.028	0.014	0.045	0.225
Vessels, diesel	0.003	0.013	0.004	0.000	0.001	0.021
Vessels, residual oil	0.007	0.057	0.009	0.000	0.000	0.073
Vessels, gasoline	0.000	0.000	0.000	0.000	0.001	0.001
Gas handling evaporation loss	0.000	0.000	0.000	0.000	0.185	0.185
						8.222

as determined by Babcock and Nagda, to the Barrett-Waddell estimate produces
a total damage figure of $18.28 billion. This figure represents an estimate of
total damages for 1970. Our estimate of total damages for 1973 is found by
adjusting this figure for inflation. This produces a figure of $21 billion per
year damages in 1973.

Estimates of yearly damage from transportation pollutants may
now be made by applying the percentage damage contributions to the estimate
of total damages. These are shown in Tables A-6 through A-8.

**Table A-7.   Damages In Chicago SMSA—Assumes All Damages
in SMSA (Pindex) (Millions)**

	PM	OS_x	NO_x	CO	HC	Total
Light-duty gasoline vehicles	6.3	2.1	34.7	18.9	68.3	129.2
Heavy-duty gasoline vehicles	0.0	0.0	6.3	2.1	11.6	20.0
Off highway gasoline	0.0	0.0	1.1	1.1	2.1	3.2
Diesel, on highway	1.1	1.1	0.0	0.0	1.1	11.6
Diesel, off highway	0.1	0.0	0.0	0.0	0.0	1.1
Diesel, train	1.1	2.1	0.0	0.0	1.1	7.4
Airplanes	1.1	1.1	0.0	0.0	1.1	5.3
Vessels	–	–	–	–	–	1.1
Gas handling evaporation loss	0.0	0.0	0.0	0.0	7.4	7.4
Total	9.5	6.3	55.7	22.1	92.4	185.9

Table A-8. Damages In Chicago SMSA—Assumes 67 Percent of All Damages in SMSA (Pindex) (Millions)

	PM	SO_x	NO_x	CO	HC	Total
Light-duty gasoline vehicles	4.2	1.4	23.2	12.7	45.8	86.6
Heavy-duty gasoline vehicles	0.0	0.0	4.2	1.4	7.8	13.4
Off highway gasoline	0.0	0.0	0.7	0.7	1.4	2.1
Diesel, on highway	0.7	0.7	0.0	0.0	0.7	7.8
Diesel, off highway	0.1	0.0	0.0	0.0	0.0	0.7
Diesel, train	0.7	1.4	0.0	0.0	0.7	5.0
Airplanes	0.7	0.7	0.0	0.0	0.7	3.6
Vessels	–	–	–	–	–	0.7
Gas handling evaporation loss	0.0	0.0	0.0	0.0	5.0	5.0
Total	6.4	4.2	37.3	14.8	61.9	124.6

Table A-9. Chicago SMSA Damages from Transportation—Assumes All Damages in SMSA Areas (composite index, in millions)

Type of Vehicle	PM	SO_x	NO_x	CO	HC	Total
Light-duty gasoline vehicles	$3.2	$ 3.4	$20.7	$6.9	$19.6	$53.8
Heavy-duty gasoline vehicles	2.4	0.3	3.6	1.9	3.3	9.3
Light-duty gasoline vehicles (off highway)	0.1	0.1	0.5	0.5	0.7	1.8
Heavy-duty diesel	0.4	1.5	5.6	0.2	0.2	8.0
Diesel, off highway	0.1	0.2	0.8	0.0	0.0	1.1
Diesel, rail	0.9	4.2	1.3	0.1	0.3	6.8
Air, military	0.1	0.0	0.0	0.0	0.0	0.1
Air, civil	0.0	0.0	0.0	0.0	0.0	0.1
Air, commercial	1.1	0.4	0.3	0.1	0.5	2.4
Vessels, diesel	0.0	0.1	0.0	0.0	0.0	0.2
Vessels, residual oil	0.1	0.6	0.1	0.0	0.0	0.8
Vessels, gasoline	0.0	0.0	0.0	0.0	0.0	0.0
Gas handling evaporation loss	0.0	0.0	0.0	0.0	1.9	1.9
Total	$8.4	$10.8	$32.9	$9.7	$ 2.65	$86.3

Table A-10. Chicago SMSA Damages from Transportation—Assumes 67 Percent of Damages in Urban Area (composite index, in millions)

Type of Vehicle	PM	SO_x	NO_x	CO	HC	Total
Light-duty gasoline vehicles	$2.1	$2.3	$13.9	$14.6	$13.1	$36.0
Heavy-duty gasoline vehicles	1.6	0.2	2.4	1.3	2.2	6.2
Light-duty gasoline vehicles (off highway)	0.0	0.1	0.3	0.3	0.5	1.2
Heavy-duty diesel	0.3	1.0	3.8	0.1	0.1	5.4
Diesel, off highway	0.1	0.1	0.5	0.0	0.0	0.7
Diesel, rail	0.1	2.8	0.9	0.1	0.2	4.6
Air, military	0.1	0.0	0.0	0.0	0.0	0.1
Air, civil	0.0	0.0	0.0	0.0	0.0	0.1
Air, commercial	0.7	0.3	0.2	0.1	0.3	1.6
Vessels, diesel	0.0	0.1	0.0	0.0	0.0	0.1
Vessels, residual oil	0.1	0.4	0.1	0.0	0.0	0.5
Vessels, gasoline	0.0	0.0	0.0	0.0	0.0	0.0
Gas handling evaporation loss	0.0	0.0	0.0	0.0	1.3	1.3
Total	$5.6	$7.2	$22.0	$ 6.5	$ 1.8	$57.8

Appendix B

Mass Transit Cost Model

A.P. Hurter

The information obtained from the modal split model must be translated into the maximum flow past the CBD cordon on each mass transit route. The costs on each route are then related to the maximum flow. This section begins with a description and "justification" for the cost model employed and concludes with a description and "justification" of a scheme for the translation of modal split results into the maximum traffic flow corridors. The cost model is based on the work of Morlok et al.[2] [1]

The purpose of the model is the estimation of changes in total system costs resulting from small changes in operations such as schedules, train lengths and the like. The model is only concerned with changes in cost as a result of scheduling changes, meaning that only variable costs are included. The inputs to the model are: headway, length of route, passenger traffic, wage rates and vehicle costs on a route-by-route basis.

Relationships between system outputs (headway, capacity) and input requirements (vehicles, operators) are necessary. Three types of inputs are considered: vehicles (buses or rail cars), crews or operators, and vehicle miles of travel. Vehicles and crews are treated explicitly because it was found that these items represent a large portion of potential costs changes resulting from peak period operational changes. For example, on a nine mile (one-way) bus route on which a vehicle can make one round trip during each peak period, the cost saving from removing one vehicle is $94 per day, of which $32 per day represents the cost of bus ownership, $47 per day wages and benefits to the operator, and $15 per day, miscellaneous other costs. The removal leads to deterioration of service, which perhaps leads to a decline in overall ridership. These secondary effects are not considered here.

The cost data used are those presented in the study by Morlok et al. The data were obtained from standard transportation accounting records. In

1. E. Morlok, W. Kulash, and H. Vandersypen, *Final Report: The Effect of Reduce Fare Plans for the Elderly on Transit System Routes* (Northeastern University Transportation Center Research Report, March 1971).

developing the bus cost model the following notation is employed:

f = peak unidirectional passenger flow past the maximum loading point taken to be the CBD cordon, in rides per hour

h_i = headway during period i (minutes per vehicle) with
$i = 1 \rightarrow$ weekday peak, $i = 2 \rightarrow$ weekday morning base,
$i = 3 \rightarrow$ weekday midday base, $i = 4 \rightarrow$ weekday evening base
$i = 5 \rightarrow$ Saturday, $i = 6 \rightarrow$ Sunday and holidays

D_i = length of period i in hours—i.e., the length of the morning or evening rush period

k = capacity of bus in passengers per bus

L = total one-way route length in miles

v_j = vehicle speed in miles per hour where $j = 1 \rightarrow$ weekday peak and $j = 2 \rightarrow$ all other

Values for v_j must be obtained empirically for the routes under study. They should include minimum layover times as well as vehicle running times. However, v_j is not to include layover times in excess of the minimum determined by labor agreement, due to scheduling mismatches, etc. Therefore, average actual speeds, including layovers, will generally be less than v_j.

s_j = vehicle slowness in minimum per mile = $(1/v_j)(60)$

C_1 = annual cost per vehicle ($ per vehicle) = $5078

C_2 = cost per vehicle mile ($ per vehicle mile) = $0.423

C_3 = cost per operator day, weekdays ($ per operator day) = $41.13

C_4 = cost per operator day, Saturdays ($ per operator day)

C_5 = cost per operator day, Sundays ($ per operator day)

The maximum traffic flow f must satisfy the physical constraint $f \leqslant 60\, k/h_1$. Further, if q is the actual capacity provided, $q = 60\, k/h_1 \geqslant f$.

The round trip time for a bus is $2Ls/60$ hours. Each time it passes the CBD cordon it takes k passengers with it, assuming it is loaded to capacity. It does this once every round trip. During a rush period, this bus carries $D_1 k/2 1s/60$ passengers where $[D_1/2 1s/60]$ is the number of round trips it can make if it is the first bus out in the rush period. Suppose that the scheduling and the definition of the rush period are such that $f/1$ buses per hour pass the CBD cordon throughout the D_1 period. Then, some of the buses must have left the terminal away from the CBD before the so-called rush period actually began. Then $D_1 k/2Ls/60$ can be interpreted as the number of trips past the CBD cordon the average bus can make during the rush period of D_1 hours. The total number of passengers to be transported during the rush is $D_1 f$. Consequently, the number of buses is

$$N'_b = (D_1 f)/(D_1 k/2Ls/60) = N'_b = f 2Ls/60k. \tag{B-1}$$

This is the number of buses with no scheduling mismatches and no layover times. Let the notation $<a>$ indicate the next largest integer to a plus 1. Then the number of buses required is $N_b = \langle 2Lsf/60k \rangle$. If $N'_b = 5.3, N_b = 7$.

Suppose that $[D_1/2Ls/60] < 1$ then the average bus—i.e., the bus leaving the far terminal at the start of the rush—can make only one incomplete trip during the rush period D. If each bus used passes the CBD cordon only once, then the number of buses required is $D_1 f/k = N^*_b$.

The number of buses is the total number of trips required $[D_1 f/k]$ divided by the number of trips per bus past the CBD cordon during the rush period, which is given by max $[1, D_1/2Ls/60]$. When the max is 1, $N^*_b = D_1 f/k$. Otherwise, $N'_b = 2lsf/60k$. Of course, the next largest integer plus 1 to N^*_b or N'_b is N_b.

Changes in relative fares and times will influence all bus ridership. Therefore, to compute the total change in the costs on each bus route resulting from a fare or time change, the change in vehicle-miles in each period of the day should be computed. However, the modal split analysis concentrates on rush period work-trips only. It is further assumed that all rush period riders go to the CBD in the morning and from the CBD in the evening, and only these riders are included in the modal split analysis. It follows, then, that ridership in off-peak periods must be assumed to be unaffected by the changes in fares and times, or if ridership changes, schedules and costs do not. Consequently, attention is restricted to changes in rush period vehicle miles. To the extent that a substantial portion of the ridership on a route does not travel to the CBD during the morning rush period, the modal split model will not capture the true change in ridership and the cost model will similarly incorrectly state the cost changes.

A 10 percent reserve for maintenance is added to the number of buses computed above. Therefore, $B = 1.1 (N_b)$.

The number of buses required on a route depends upon f, which is obtained from the modal split analysis and from the allocation model to be described below, and on L_1, s_1 and k which are characteristics of the route and are obtained from the bus operators. This procedure involves the assumption that comfort and convenience levels are maintained at their present levels on each route regardless of the changes in times and fares employed. If the buses are not filled to capacity when they pass the CBD cordon, substitute k' for k in the above where k' is the average number of passengers per bus in the rush period when the bus passes the CBD cordon.

Exactly the same calculations are used, with different parameter values, to arrive at the number of trains and train cars needed on a train route. An additional parameter, n_1, the number of cars per train, is required, with k being interpreted as the capacity of a car. Morlok suggests an eight percent reserve for maintenance. Then $C = 1.08n_1(N_t)$, with C the number of train cars required on the route.

Assuming 250 rush period days annually, the annual vehicle-miles for a bus route and the annual car-miles for a train route can be calculated as:

$$V_b = 250\,(2)\,(2L)N_b \text{ and}$$

$$V_c = 250\,(2)\,(2L)n_1 N_t.$$

V_b and V_c refer to the rush periods, of which there are two each day.

The computation of the number of crew-days per year on a route is more complicated, since the crews may also work, or at least be paid for, more than just the rush period. In addition, one crew may not be able to work both rush periods without overtime pay. It is assumed that the morning and evening rush periods are identical and that the morning and evening base periods are the same. The crew needs for the rush period, in addition to those needed for the base periods, are:

$$\alpha_b = N_b - \langle 2s^2 L/h^2 \rangle \text{ or}$$

$$\alpha_c = N_t - \langle 2s^2 L/h^2 \rangle$$

where the superscript 2 refers to base period parameter values. Notice that s^2 has the units of minutes per mile, L is the length of the route in miles, and h^2 is the nonrush period headway in minutes per bus or minutes per train. Then: (minutes per mile) (mile) (buses or trains per minute) = buses or trains. Thus, α is the difference between the number of vehicles and crews required for the heaviest rush period (morning or evening) and the heaviest base period. If men were hired for work rather than in accordance with union requirements, we would be finished.

However, the rush hour crew costs alone are not adequate and annual work day crew-days mut be computed. Since we have assumed that the two base periods are the same, we need not consider the hiring of extra crews which would work one base period and not the other. The time from the beginning of the morning peak to the end of the evening peak is $D_1 + D_2 + D_2 + D_1$ or $2D_1 + 2D_2$. A crew gets paid for 8 hours + 0.5 $(2D_1 + 2D_2 - 8)$. In other words, they get time and one-half for hours "worked" over eight. For purposes of the costing models, this extra pay time can be converted to "equivalent" extra crews. Then the "extra" crew-days paid for per work day are:

$$C = [8 + .5(2D_1 + 2D_s - 8)]\ (\alpha/8). \tag{B-2}$$

Crew-days per year are:

$$M_{1-4} = 250 \left\{ 2 \langle 2s^2 L/h \rangle + [8 + 0.5(2D_1 + 2D_2 - 8)]\ (\alpha/8) \right\}. \tag{B-3}$$

The procedure is the same for rail or for bus with α_c or α_b being substituted in the appropriate place along with the appropriate values of s, L, and h.

The rush period cost are:

$$\tau_k = 16{,}049\ (C) + 0.355 V_c + 81.50\ M_{1-4\ c} \qquad \text{for trains and} \tag{B-4}$$

$$\tau_b = 5078\ (B) + 0.423\ V_b + 41.33\ M_{1-4\ b} \qquad \text{for busses.} \tag{B-5}$$

These are the annual costs on each route.

Notice that M_{1-4} must be computed for each route. However, s^2 and h^2 on a particular route do not change from scenario to scenario due to the assumption that the time and cost changes do not effect nonrush period operations. Consequently, in the computation for M_{1-4}, only α changes from scenario to scenario to scenario and, in the calculation of α, only f changes from scenario to scenario. Thus, with a little algebra, τ_t and τ_b could both be expressed as functions of f with all other terms being treated as parameters. One difficulty with this procedure is the requirement of integer values for N_b and N_c, which are used in computing C, B, V_c, V_b, $M_{1-4\ c}$, and $M_{1-4\ b}$. A second difficulty is that N_b and N_c depend upon whether the route is a long one or a short one relative to the round trip times.

The cost coefficients employed in the equations for τ_t and τ_b are taken from the Morlok report. These cost coefficients should be revised to reflect costs in 1973. However, our primary interest is in cost differences between operations dictated by a time and fare change scenario and the present. If inflation has affected all cost items equally, then the true cost difference and the computed cost difference will themselves differ only by the inflation factor. Again, in keeping with the expected accuracy of the ridership figures as generated by the modal split model, no attempt will be made to revise the cost coefficients used in calculating τ_t and τ_b. In addition, the same coefficients will be used whether the mass transit line is operated by the CTA or by a private company.

ALLOCATION MODEL

The modal split model yields ridership by mode for CATS zones. Let Q_{ji} be the present number of work-trips by all modes in CATS zone i in ring j. This information is assumed to be known. Compute

$$R_j = \sum_{i=1}^{n_j} Q_{ji},$$

the total number of work-trips with origins in ring j. For each modal split scenario and for the present obtain the total number of CBD work-trips in ring j from the modal split model. Call this number r_j. For each ring and each scenario, including the present, compute $W_j = r_j/R_j$, the fraction of all work-trips in ring j that are CBD trips. Then compute $q_{ji} = W_j Q_{ji}$, the number of CBD-bound work-trips in zone i of ring j. From the modal split results obtain the number of CBD work-trips in ring j by bus (B_j), by train (T_j) and by auto (A_j). This calculation is done for all rings and for each scenario. Then for each ring and each scenario including the present compute $X_j = B_j/r_j$; $Y_j = T_j/r_j$; $Z_j = A_j/r_j$. X_j is the fraction of all CBD work-trips from ring j by bus, with Y_j and Z_j similarly defined for train and automobile trips. For each zone compute $b_{ji} = X_j q_{ji}$, the number of bus trips from zone i in ring j to the CBD. The train and auto trips from zone i in ring j to the CBD are respectively t_{ji} and a_{ji}.

  At this point, the number of trips from each zone by each mode for each scenario has been computed and labeled b_{ji}, t_{ji}, and a_{ji}. This ridership must now be allocated to bus and train routes. Only routes to the CBD are included. Consider a map of existing bus routes (a similar procedure is followed for train routes). First, identify those routes which go to the CBD. The bus lines to the CBD will pass through some of the zones on the map. "Stations" are arbitrarily positioned along each route, one in each zone through which a bus route to the CBD passes. Some zones will have stations on more than a single route since more than one bus route passes through that zone. In this case, the bus ridership from the zone in question is equally divided among the bus lines passing through that zone. There will be some zones through which no CBD-bound bus lines pass. Bus ridership from such zones is then allocated to the closest station to the zone in question. Train routes are treated similarly.

  The rush period ridership at each station can now be computed. At this point in the process, the modal split results have been translated into rush period ridership entering bus and train lines at each of the stations. The use of these artificial stations ignores aspects of access to bus or train routes from the various zones. Each rider is assumed to have access to all modes of travel. Let $^kB_{ji}$ be the total rush period bus traffic to the CBD on route k as work-trips boarding in the morning or leaving in the evening from the station in zone i of ring j. We are interested in traffic past the CBD cordon on each route—more specifically the maximum flow past the CBD cordon on each route.

A complete model might generate the time distribution of traffic at each station during the rush period. Let S_k be the set of stations located on route k. Then the total rush period ridership on route k is $jieS_k{}^kB_{ji}$. If we suppose that the rush period is divided into, say 15 minute periods $p = 1, \ldots, P,$ and we let γ_p be the proportion of rush period CBD riders who arrive in time interval $p,$ then $\gamma_p \Sigma j, ieS_k{}^kB_{ji}$ is the number of riders on route k passing the CBD cordon during time interval p of the rush priod. Then the maximum flow rate on route k past the CBD cordon would be

$$k_f = \max_p \left\{ \gamma_p \Sigma jieS_k{}^kB_{ji} \right\}. \tag{B-6}$$

Of course, k_f must be computed for each route, bus and rail, and for each scenario. In these calculations it is assumed that the time distribution of the total traffic to the CBD is known, yielding the γ_p values, but the time distribution on each line, or in rings and zones, is not known.

The procedure just outlined was revised slightly in practice. A regular CTA transit map was obtained. One inch grids corresponding to CATS zones were superimposed on this map. All bus routes leading to the CBD were traced on the map. There were 36 bus routes. The zones covered in each ring were identified from the map. The modal split results do not include ring one (closest to the CBD), which includes 14 zones. Projections were made to include this ring, and these are included in the following sections.

The rush period scheduling of the CTA is not indicated on the CTA schedules and consequently the necessary headway values for the various routes is unknown. An approximation to the present values of k_f on each route has been employed wherein $k_{f_o} = 60k/k_{h_1}$. Here, the subscript o indicates the present.

Currently available data on the time distribution of CBD work-trips in the morning do not permit the calculation of γ_p for each 15 minute portion of the rush period. Therefore, the assumption is made that each car of a train or a bus that passes the CBD cordon during the rush period is filled to its capacity k. Then, the headway during the rush period on route a is determined and an estimate made of the maximum flow past the cordon: $a_{f_o} = 60k/h_1$. This procedure is less satisfying than that described earlier for the calculation of a_{f_o}, but was used in this analysis because of data limitations. Once a_{f_o} was computed for each route, the maximum flows on the route a under conditions of scenario q was computed as follows:

$$a_{f_q} = a_{f_0} [(\Sigma jieS_a{}^{aBji}) \, q \, / \, (jieS_a{}^{aBji})o] .$$
(B-7)

The cost model described at the beginning of this section is used with the values of a_{f_q} to compute costs.

Notice that values of a_{Bji} must be obtained for each scenario using the modal split and allocation models just described. The identity of the stations on each bus or rail route—i.e., the elements of S_a—will not change from one scenario to the next. The values of Q_{ji}, R_j, r_j, W_j, q_{ji}, and q^{aji} also depend on the scenario (q) being considered. Since k_{Bji} is the fraction of b_{ji} assigned to route k, plus any contributions from other zones (b_{rs}), where the ridership in zone s of ring r is assigned to the station in zone s in ring r, k_{Bji} changes from scenario to scenario. It can only be obtained through application of the allocation model for each scenario. The same is true for k_{Tji} which is the total rush period, work-trip rail traffic to the CBD on route k boarding in the morning or leaving in the evening from the station in zone i of ring j. It is related to t_{ji} in the same way b_{ji} is related to k_{Bji}. Since t_{ji} and b_{ji} depend on the scenario, we should more correctly have written: q^{bji}, q^{kBji}, q^{tji}, and q^{kTji}.

COST CALCULATIONS AND RESULTS

The basic map used was a CTA map showing bus and CTA train routes. This map covers Chicago and also includes such suburbs as Evanston, Skokie, Lincoln-wood, Morton Grove, Park Ridge, Des Plaines, Maywood, Crestwood, etc. When bus calculations are made, only rings two to five are included since long bus trips are unlikely. The CTA bus lines end at the Chicago city limits. For train calculations, portions of ring six are also included.

Recall that Q_{ji} is the present number of work trips by all modes in CATS zone i in ring j. These data are obtained from independent sources. Notice that r_1 data were not available. The r_j and B_j figures used to compute b_{ji} are obtained from the modal split analysis. However, the modal split work does not include ring one. Ring one does contain zones which are not in the CBD. Values of X_1 and W_1 were estimated by plotting X_j and W_j, $j = 2, \ldots, 6$ and linearly extrapolating the graph to estimate X_1 and W_1. Similar data must be prepared for rail and auto trips and the b_{ji}, t_{ji} and a_{ji} developed for each scenarios. These data are available but will not be repeated here. They can be derived from the modal split estimates and the values of Q_{ji}.

The values of b_{ji} and t_{ji} are assigned to one of 36 bus routes or one of 12 train routes respectively. There are several possibilities for each b_{ji}. It is either assigned to a particular bus route, partially assigned to the bus route or not assigned to the bus route in question. This procedure has been outlined in the section on the allocation model. The values of the b_{ji} and t_{ji} will change from scenario to scenario but their allocation to bus and train routes will not change. That is, whether b_{ji} contributes to k_{Bji} and to $\Sigma_{jieS_k}{}^{kBji}$

does not depend on the scenario under consideration although the amount of its contribution may vary from scenario to scenario. The values of $k_{B_{ji}}$ must be computed for each scenario and each route and this requires that values for b_{ji} must be computed for each scenario as they were computed for the present as shown in the preceding tables. Once the allocation scheme is determined, S_k and $k_{B_{ji}}$ can be determined and so can $\Sigma_{ji \epsilon S_k}{}^{kB_{ji}}$ for the kth route. Since $k_{f_o} = 60k/h_1$,

$$k_{f_q} = k_{f_o} \; [(\Sigma_{ji \epsilon S_k}{}^{kB_{ji}})q/(\Sigma_{ji \epsilon S_k}{}^{kB_{ji}})_o] \; . \tag{B-8}$$

Of course, similar calculations are required for the train routes.

The calculations leading to the k_{f_q} values, the maximum flows on route k for scenario q, are thus straightforward but tedious. A sample for bus route 131 under present condtions is presented to clarify the procedure. The route length L is six miles and the length of the rush period D is two hours. The one-way trip rush period running time is 45 minutes. The rush period head-way, h_1 is five minutes. The capacity of a bus, k, is taken to be 70. Then

$$131_{f_o} = 60k/h_1 = (60)\,(70)/5 = 840 \text{ passengers per hour} \tag{B-9}$$

on bus route 131 past the CBD cordon during the rush period. Now

$$v_1 = 6/.75 = 8\text{mph so } s_1 = (1/8)\,(60) = 7.5 \text{ minutes per mile.} \tag{B-10}$$

It takes

$$2Ls_1/60 = 2(6)\,(7.5)/60 = 1.5 \text{ hours} \tag{B-11}$$

for a vehicle to make a round trip. The mas $[1, D/2Ls_1/60] = $ mas $[1, 60 \times 2/(2)\,(6)\,(7.5)] = $ mas $[1,1.33] = 1.33$ trips per rush period by the average bus on route 131. Therefore, the number of buses required is

$$N_b' = 2Ls_1 k_{f_o}/60k = N_b' = (2)\,(6)\,(7.5)\,(840)/(60)\,(70) = 18.05. \tag{B-12}$$

Then $N_b = \langle 18.05 \rangle = 20$ buses. The requirement of a ten percent reserve for maintenance means that the number of buses required for route 131 is $131_{B_o} = 22$. The annual number of vehicle miles, $V_b = 250\,(2)\,(2L)N_b = (250)\,(2)\,(2)\,(6)\,(20) = 1000\,(120) = 120{,}000$ vehicle miles per year.

The headway during the base period is $h_2 = 7.5$ minutes while the one-way running time is 37 minutes. Then $v_2 = (6/37)\,(60) = 9.73$ mph and $s_2 = (1/9.73)\,(60) = 6.16$ minutes per mile. Buses needed for the weekday base period are

Table B-1.   Results Table

Policy Measure	No.	ΔT	ΔC	Daily Auto Rides	Daily Bus Rides	Daily Rail Rides	Daily All Rides	Change Auto
No change	S_0	0	0	26,956	49,674	223,999	300,579	0
45¢ fare decrease	S_1	0	+.45	15,243	59,410	225,926	300,579	−11,762
90¢ fare decrease	S_2	0	+.90	8,190	67,721	224,668	300,579	−18,771
9:00 parking increase	S_3	0	+2.00	461	76,055	224,063	300,579	−26,500
5 min. reduction in auto travel time	S_4	−5	0	30,625	47,624	220,329	300,579	+3,669
55¢ decrease in parking fees parking	S_5	0	−.55	48,091	34,060	218,430	300,579	+21,135
15 min. increase in cars travel time	S_6	+10	0	21,669	51,066	227,666	300,579	−5,287
Simultaneous use of S_5 and S_6	S_7	+10	−.55	37,942	34,792	227,263	300,579	+10,986
25¢ fare increase	S_8	0	−.25	37,706	40,639	222,006	300,579	+10,750

$$\langle 2 s^2 L/^2 h \rangle = \langle (2)\,(6.16)\,(6)/7.5 \rangle = \langle 9.87 \rangle = 11. \tag{B-13}$$

Then $\alpha = 20 - 11 = 9$. The difference between the number of buses and crews required for the rush period and the base period is nine. Then

$$M_{1-4} = 250 \left\{ 2\langle s^2 L/^2 h \rangle + [8 + 0.5(2D_1 + 2D_2 - 8)\,(\alpha/8) \right\} . \tag{B-14}$$

since $D_1 = 2$ hours, $D_2 = 3.5$ hours and $\alpha = 9$, $M_{1-4} = 250\{32.69\}$ or $M_{1-4} = 8{,}172$ annual crew days. Now:

$$T_b = 5078(22)+).423(120{,}000) + 41.33(8172) = \$500{,}225 \tag{B-15}$$

which is the estimate of the annual costs of interest on route 131. The reader is reminded that no claim has been made for the accuracy of T_b as an estimate of the annual costs of operating route 131. Some costs not affected by the scenarios were purposely omitted. Concentration on rush period figures further distorts the value of T_b. It is the difference between $(131_{T_b})_o$ present times and costs and $(131_{T_b})_q$ under scenario q that is of interest here.

Change Bus	Change Rail	Bus Cost	Rail Cost	Total Cost	Change Bus	Change Rail	Change Total
0	0	20,354,714	47,372,928	67,727,642	0	0	0
-9,788	+1,928	23,322,868	48,362,056	71,684,924	+2,968,154	+989,128	3,957,282
+18,098	+670	25,125,110	48,038,971	73,341,923	+4,770,396	+666,043	5,614,419
+26,432	+65	26,786,441	47,372,928	74,159,369	+6,431,727	0	6,431,727
0	-3,669	20,354,714	46,353,014	66,707,728	0	-1,019,914	-1,019,914
-15,564	-5,569	16,397,464	46,875,226	63,272,690	-3,957,250	-497,702	-4,454,952
+1,442	+3,668	21,330,653	48,041,664	69,372,317	+975,939	+668,736	1,644,675
-14,832	+3,264	16,602,726	49,288,761	65,891,687	-3,751,988	+1,916,033	-1,835,955
-8,985	-1,993	20,354,714	47,249,760	66,604,474	-2,122,142	-123,168	-3,245,310

Table B-1 shows the results of the above described sequence of calculations. Consider the sequence of scenarios $S5, S8, S1, S2, S3$, wherein the cost difference changes in favor of mass transit as we move from $S5$ to $S3$. When a \$2 parking fee increase is instituted, resulting in a \$2 one trip increase in the cost difference between automobile and mass transit, almost all automobile traffic switches to bus. Throughout all the scenarios, the change in rail ridership is small relative to changes in bus and automobile traffic. When the dominance of rail, which takes 73.5 percent of the present ridership, is considered, the small change in rail ridership is even more surprising. The maximum change in rail ridership occurs in response to $S5$ where a decrease of 5,569 in riders using rail occurs. This is a $(5.569 \times 10^3 \times 10^2)$ 92.24×10^5) = 2.5 percent decrease in rail ridership. The unexpected, modest change in rail ridership, regardless of which scenario is under consideration, warrants an emphasis on bus versus auto.

It is interesting to note that when changes in travel time differences rather than changes in cost differences are emphasized ($S6, S4$) automobile and rail travel seem to be in competition, with only minimal influence on bus travel. Referring to the modal split results for $S4$ we can observe that the largest change in rail ridership, as projected by the modal split model, occurred in ring four. The same is true of *S*6. Ring four just skirts the city limits, with approximately 75 percent of its ridership from within the city. In this area rail service is readily accessible, especially the CTA rail lines. From points in ring four, a five or ten minute increase in automobile travel time to the CBD undoubtedly represents a substantial percentage increase in trip times.

In interpreting these results, the mechanics of the modal split model must be kept in mind. The peculiar result that when travel times on the different modes are changed automobiles and rail compete for traffic while when fares or costs for the different modes are changed busses and automobiles compete must be explained with reference to the modal split model.

The sequence of scenarios dealing with changes in fare differences yields results which are summarized in Figure B-1. This figure clearly indicates the substitution of bus for automobile travel as the cost of using the latter rises relative to the cost of using the former. These results cannot be taken too seriously for the more extreme cases such as *S*3. Its difficult to imagine that

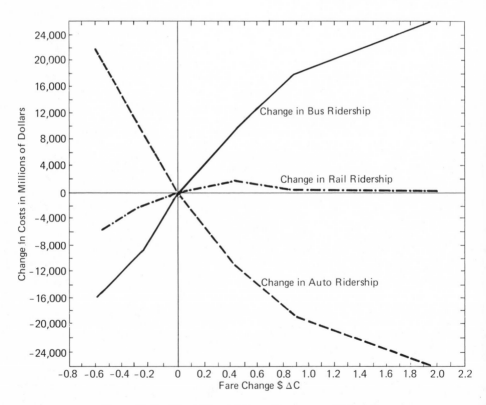

Figure B-1. The Effect of Fare Changes on Ridership.

a $2 daily increase in parking fees would leave only 461 rush period work-trips by auto to the CBD. Even if this could be a transitory result, it would not prevail for long. Certainly the relative times of travel would shift dramatically in favor of automobiles and there would be considerable pressure to reduce parking fees on the part of lot operators faced with empty lots. In short, the modal split coefficients have been assumed to be stable over what appears to be a very wide range of the independent variables ΔC and ΔT. It would not be surprising to discover that this assumption is violated. However, with the data and other information now available to us, no corrections to the projections of the table can be made.

Costs of mass transit as a function of fare changes are summarized in Figure B-2. Notice that the relationship for the bus seems to be almost linear in the range of fare changes between -.55 and +.90. Consider scenario $S6$ which involves no fare change, but does involve a ten minute increase in automobile travel time. This scenario results in $975,939 annual increase in bus operating costs. Using the figure, this is the same increase as the one which would be generated by a 15 cent fare increase. Of course, this estimate of 1.5 cents per minute as a "value of travel time" applies only when the choice is between bus and automobile.

The cost results may be shown in one further format as given in Figure B-3. The strange behavior of rail cost changes with both fare changes and ridership is also shown on Figures B-2 and B-3 where the data of Table B-1 are plotted. No ready explanation of this behavior is apparent. The behavior of cost changes on rail as a function of ridership as shown in Figure B-3 is particularly puzzling.

Some of the assumptions used to make the rail cost calculations are detailed below. Unfortunately, they do not provide a complete explanation for the cost behavior illustrated in Figures B-2 and B-3. The general cost assumptions and those used for the bus cost calculations were outlined in an earlier section.

1. The cost analysis is limited to the costs incurred by the train companies while operating within specific geographic boundaries. The ends of the line for the CTA routes all fall within these boundaries. The ends of the line for the commuter trains generally extend well beyond these geographic boundaries and thus the total costs of operating these routes is not reflected in these calculations.
2. The geographic limits for the rail cost calculation are different from those used for the bus calculations. Therefore, the number of CATS zones included differs from those used in the calculations of bus line costs. In making the bus cost calculations, the costs referred to CTA buses which operate in Chicago. The train costs, on the other hand, include commuter trains and additional zones. For the bus case 222 CATS zones were included, while in the rail case 381 CATS zones were included.

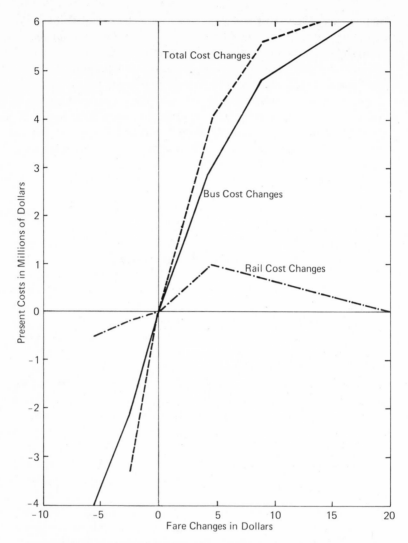

Figure B-2. Mass Transit Costs: Differences from Present as Functions of Fare Changes.

3. One tenet of the modal split model is that all riders have access to all modes. Thus, it has been assumed that the percentage of train riders in each zone of a ring is the same regardless of the distance of the rail line from the zone.
4. The train car capacities are seating capacities. For CTA rail cars they are taken to be 50—i.e., $k = 50$—while for commuter trains they are 150.
5. The number of cars per train (n) was obtained for each line. When the number of cars varied during the rush period, an average value was used.

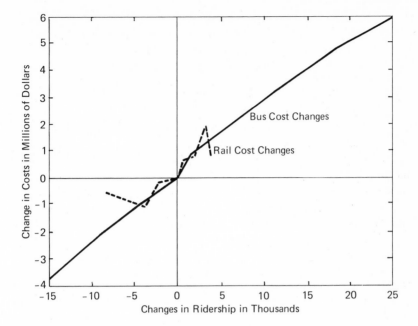

Figure B–3.

6. The capacity of a bus (k) was taken to be 70 and it includes both seated and some standing passengers. This figure is used by the CTA during the rush period when they attempt to determine the number of buses needed on a route.

Again referring to Table B-1, it may be helpful to recall the interpretations of the scenarios. For example, consider the interpretation of a 45 cent fare decrease on mass transit. Recall that the modal split model is run three times for each ring using three equations: (1) car-bus, (2) car-train and (3) car-other. The third equation establishes the percent automobile for each ring. The first and second equations establish the split of the remaining percentage between rail and bus, through a normalization procedure described earlier, in each ring. Four independent variables are used in each of the three equations. I, the average income in each ring and D, the distance to the CBD from points in each ring, do not change from scenario to scenario. ΔT, the time by automobile minus the time by mass transit and ΔC, the cost by automobile minus the cost by mass transit, do change from scenario to scenario, ring to ring and equation to equation.

Let ΔC_{tj} be the present difference in costs: automobile costs to CBD from ring j minus train costs to CBD from ring j under present conditions. ΔC^1_{tj} is the difference under scenario S_1 (45 cent fare decrease). Then ΔC^1_{tj}

$= \Delta C^{o}_{tj} + 45$, all $j = 2, \ldots 6$. Also $\Delta C^{1}_{bj} = \Delta C^{o}_{bj} + 45$, all $j = 2, \ldots, 6$. These values of ΔC^{1}_{bj} and ΔC^{1}_{tj} are used in the first two equations for ring j ($j = 2, \ldots, 6$) to compute ridership for S_1. In the third equation some kind of average of ΔC^{1}_{bj} and ΔC_{tj} must be used. Call it ΔC_{dj}. Then, $\Delta C^{1}_{dj} = \Delta C_{dj} + 45$ is used in the third equation. The point is that the modal split analysis for ring j under scenario S_1 is run using ΔC^{1}_{dj}, ΔC^{1}_{bj} and ΔC^{1}_{tj} together. The 45 cent fare decrease applies to all forms of mass transit at once.

Not only is the difference between automobile and rail and between automobile and bus costs altered from scenario to scenario, so is the cost of rail relative to the cost of bus travel. For example, if bus fare is 46 cents and rail fare is 90 cents from some zones to the CBD then a 45 cent fare reduction on mass transit alters the ratio of bus to rail costs from 46/90 to 1/45. Under ordinary treatments of consumer choice theory, one would expect a substitution of bus for rail since rail becomes relatively more expensive. Looking at the rail ridership figures realted to $S1$, $S2$ and $S3$ there is evidence that as the fare decrease gets larger, a larger and larger proportion of those riders switching from automobiles to mass transit choose bus rather than rail. Suppose $\Delta C_{tj} = \$2$ and $\Delta C_{bj} = \$3$. Then $\Delta C_{tj} = \$2.45$ and $\Delta C_{bj} = \$3.45$. The ratio is $2.00/3.00 < 2.45/3.45$, indicating that rail is more costly relative to bus under $S1$ rather than $S0$.

Again, consider the results with respect to rail ridership and costs associated with scenarios $S4$ and $S5$. Table B–1 indicates that the five minute reduction in automobile travel time associated with $S4$ results in no change in bus ridership but a decrease of 3,669 in rail ridership accompanied by a decrease of $1,019,914 in rail costs. However, the 55 cent decrease in parking fees associated with $S5$ results in a 15,564 decrease in bus ridership, and a 5,569 decrease in rail ridership accompanied by a $497,702 decrease in rail costs. A possible explanation for this result, although it can only be considered speculation, is that when the trip time is decreased by five minutes it has most influence on riders close to the CBD perhaps in rings one, two and three. This is because a five minute reduction in a 20 minute trip is more important than a five minute decrease in a two hour trip. Since the closer rings are less dominated by rail travel than those farther out, a substantial change in ridership from these rings might lead to a dramatic increase in the number of trains and train cars required. This effect may be accentuated by the integer requirements on the number of cars and on the number of trains. On the other hand, the 55 cent decrease in parking fees leads to a substantial decrease in both rail and bus ridership. It is reasonable to assume that in the closer rings the major influence is on bus riders while in the outer rings it is on rail ridership. Then, under $S4$ the decrease in rail ridership takes place from rings one through three while under $S5$ it takes place in the rings farther out. Since the travel from rings farther out is already dominated by rail travel, even substantial decreases or increases in ridership may not result in large changes in the trains and train cars required and consequently the cost changes are relatively modest. This is presumed to be the case under the 55 cent parking fee decrease of $S5$. A modest change in rail ridership from the closer rings where rail is not as dominant might lead to substantial changes in rail trains required and consequently in rail costs. This is presumed to be the case with the five minute travel time reduction of $S4$.

Again referring to Table B-1, a simultaneous 55 cent decrease in parking fee and a ten minute increase in auto travel time ($S7$) results in an increase of 3,264 in rail ridership and $1,916,033 in rail costs. A ten minute increase in automobile travel time alone ($S6$) results in a 3,668 increase in rail ridership and a $668,736 increase in rail costs. The 55 cent decrease in parking fees alone ($S5$) results in a 5,569 reduction in rail ridership with a $497,702 reduction in rail cost. Notice that under $S5$ bus ridership decreases 15,564, under $S6$ it increases 1,442 and under $S7$ it decreases 14,832.

Under $S7$ bus ridership decreases while rail ridership increases. This must be presumed to be a phenomenon taking place in the rings closer to the CBD where changes in rail ridership seem to be very expensive. Thus the ratio of rail cost to rail ridership change should be expected to be high for $S7$ as shown. Under $S5$ both rail and bus ridership fall dramatically and it is to be expected that the rail change takes place in the more distant rings so that, according to the earlier argument, the ratio of rail cost change to rail ridership change is lower than under $S7$. Under $S6$ both rail and bus ridership increase. With the presumption that rail changes take place primarily in the outer rings the ratio of cost change to ridership change should be relatively low.

Under $S7$, the modal split results indicate substantial increases in rail ridership in the three closest rings, while decreases in rail ridership under $S7$ are shown for rings five and six. Under $S7$ bus ridership declined in all rings. Notice that increases in rail ridership in rings one, two and three more than balance the decreases in rings five and six. Thus, there is a shift toward auto in all rings under $S7$ accompanied by a shift toward rail in rings one, two and three. This latter shift means a shift to CTA rail ridership close to the CBD which is the area where changes in rail ridership result in relatively large changes in rail costs. The reason for the apparent shift of some bus passengers to rail under $S7$ is not clear.

These "explanations" are speculative at best. They are presented here as suggestive rather than definitive. This section on rail costs will now be concluded with the presentation of a simple calculation for rail costs.

CTA Rail Route to Des Plaines (Route CM)

Running time: rush 48 minutes; base 46 minutes

Car per train: rush n_1 = 6 cars; base n_2 = 2 cars

Headway: rush $h_1 = 3$ minutes; base $h_2 = 4$ minutes

$L = 8$ miles,

$k = 50$, and

$D_1 = 2$ hours

$f_o = 60n_1 k/h_1 = (60)(6)(50)/3 = 6{,}000$ passengers per hour

$v_1 = 8/48/60 = 10$mph; $s_1 = (1/10)(60) = 6$ minutes per mile

It takes $2Ls_1/60 = (2)(8)(6)/60 = 1.6$ hours for a train to make a round trip.
The max $[1, D_1/2Ls_1/60] = \max[1,(60)(2)/(2)(8)(6) = \max[1, 1.25] = 1.25$
trips per rush period by the average rush period train on route CM. Therefore,
the number of trains required is

$$N_t^1 = 2Ls_1^k f_o/60kn_1 = (2)(8)(6)(6000)/(60)(50)(6)$$

$$= N_t^1 = (10)(8)(2)/(5) = 32. \tag{B-16}$$

Then:

$N_t = \langle 32 \rangle = 33$ trains,

$C = 1.08\,(6)(33) = 214$ rail cars during the rush period on route CM, and

$V_c = (250)(2)(16)(6)(33) = 1{,}585{,}000$ car miles per year.

During the base periods, $N_2 = 8/46/60 = 10.42$mph and $s_2 = (1/10.42)(60) = 5.75$ minutes per mile. Trains needed for the weekday base period
are

$$\langle 2s_2 L/h_2 \rangle = \langle 2(5.75)(8)/4 \rangle = \langle 23 \rangle = 24 \text{ and } \alpha = 33 - 24 = 9. \tag{B-17}$$

Therefore, operator days are:

$$M_{1-4} = 250\{(2)(24) + 8 + 0.5\,(4 + 7 - 8)(9/8)\} = 250\{48 + 9.69\}$$

$$= M_{1-4}\,250(57.69) = 14{,}400 \text{ annual crew days on route CM.} \tag{B-18}$$

Now

$$T_t = (16,049)(214) + .355(1,585,000) + 81.5(14,400) =$$

$$T_t = 3,440,000 + 562,00 + 1,172,000 =$$

$$T_t = \$5,174,000 \tag{B-19}$$

BENEFITS

Returning to Table B-1, consider the interpretations possible for scenario $S1$. In response to a 45 cent fare reduction for a one-way trip on both bus and rail mass transit, 11,762 fewer auto trips to the CBD during the rush period are projected. Ninety-two percent of those switching from automobiles went to bus, raising bus costs by \$2,968,154 per year. If it is assumed that work-trip automobile users average 1.5 passengers per car, then under S_o we have: $(26,956)/(1.5) = 17,950$ automobile trips to CBD each day. In 1972 the number of vehicle miles per day in the CBD generated by taxicabs was 252,935, which was 22 percent of the total. The total number of vehicle miles generated in the CBD each day is then $2.529 \times 10^5/2.2 \times 10^{-1} = 1.15 \times 10^6$. Assume that private automobiles amount for 70 percent and therefore generate 8.06×10^5 vehicle miles per day. This would mean an average of $8.06 \times 10^5/1.79 \times 10^4 = 45$ miles per day per car in the CBD. This number seems much too high. Instead, if we assume each private car travels 10 miles per day in the CBD (five miles in and five out), and even this seems rather high, then the vehicle mile estimate must be altered to $(1.79 \times 10^4)(10) = 179,500$ vehicle miles per day.

Notice that the 1.79×10^4 is taken as the number of CBD-bound, rush period work-trips. These trips are the ones of concern to the split modal analysis. Recall the earlier assumption that all other traffic remains unaffected by the time and fare changes described in the scenarios. Therefore, 179,500 vehicle miles per day are generated in the CBD by rush period work-trips in private automobiles.

Under $S0$ then, if we assume all trips are made in 1972 cars, the rush period work-trips generate:

$$(3.54)(1.79 \times 10^5) = 6.35 \times 10^5 \text{ grams per day HC,}$$

$$(3.9 \times 10)(1.79 \times 10^5) = 6.99 \times 10^6 \text{ grams per day CO, and}$$

$$(2.7)(1.79 \times 10^5) = 4.84 \times 10^5 \text{ grams per day NO}_x.$$

With our assumption, private vehicles under S_0 generate:

$$(1.79 \times 10^5)(10^2)/(1.15 \times 10^6) = 1.56 \times 10 = 15.6 \text{ percent} \qquad \text{(B-20)}$$

of the total number of CBD vehicle miles.[2]

Under $S1$ only 15,243 person trips by automobile are projected and these will generate $[(1.524 \times 10^4)/(1.5)] \ (10) = 1.015 \times 10^5$ vehicle miles per day.

These vehicle miles generate:

$$(3.54)(1.01 \times 10^5) = 3.59 \times 10^5 \text{ grams per day HC,}$$

$$(3.9)(1.01 \times 10^5) = 3.96 \times 10^5 \text{ grams per day CO, and}$$

$$(2.7)(1.01 \times 10^5) = 2.72 \times 10^5 \text{ grams per day NO}_x.$$

The pollution emission levels in the CBD from all automotive sources under $S0$ are estimated as:

$$(6.35 \times 10^5)/(1.56 \times 10^{-1}) = 4.07 \times 10^6 \text{ grams per day HC,}$$

$$(6.99 \times 10^6)/(1.56 \times 10^{-1}) = 4.47 \times 10^7 \text{ grams per day CO, and}$$

$$(4.84 \times 10^5)/(1.56 \times 10^{-1}) = 3.1 \times 10^6 \text{ grams per day NO}_x.$$

Since private automobile work-trips account for 15.6 percent of all CBD vehicle miles based on the estimates just made, we have assumed that all vehicle miles by whatever type of vehicle generate emissions equivalent to those from 1972 cars.

The difference in emissions between $S1$ and $S0$ is:

$$(6.35 - 3.59)10^5 = 2.76 \times 10^5 \text{ grams per day HC,}$$

$$(6.99 - 3.96)10^6 = 3.03 \times 10^6 \text{ grams per day CO, and}$$

$$(4.84 - 2.72)10^5 = 2.12 \times 10^5 \text{ grams per day NO}_x.$$

The percentage reduction in CBD emissions is: 6.78 percent HC, 6.78 percent CO and 6.78 percent NO$_x$.

These percentage reductions and the cost of obtaining them should be compared to other strategies such as the various taxicab strategies. However, the absolute cost in both the taxicab and mass transit analyses are not accurate

2. A. Hurter, Benefit Table, "Report on Proposal to Use Gaseous Fuels in Chicago Taxicab Fleet" (Argonne National Laboratory: Center for Environmental Studies, Argonne, Ill., August 1973).

representations of the cost. In both cases, cost differences between alternatives were stressed, with items not expected to vary in cost between the alternatives under consideration being ignored. These ignored items could be of paramount importance in comparing a taxicab strategy with a mass transit strategy. The statement that immediate replacement of all gasoline cabs with LPG cabs and then gradual return to gasoline will cost 2.351×10^6 per year and result in an 18 percent reduction in HC, a 20 percent reduction in CO and a 0.34 percent increase in NO_x means that the cost is 2.351×10^6 per year more than the nonintervention policy $S0$.[1]

    Comparisons of this sort can and should be made. However, before additional calculations are made, confirmation of the estimates used for total CBD pollution and that contributed by private vehicles during rush periods is needed.

    One step toward putting the taxicab and mass transit studies on the same basis is to recalculate the total CBD emissions directly from the benefits table of the taxicab study. Again, it was assumed that the entire fleet of vehicles contributing to CBD emissions consists of 1972 automobiles. Since taxicabs generate 22 percent of the total vehicle miles, an estimate of the percentage reduction in total CBD emission due to taxicab policies, or, alternatively, the percentage reduction assuming all other vehicle traffic is done in 1972, 1973 or 1974 cars, all of which have the same emission characteristics, is:

(emission reduction grams per day) $(.22)$ (10^2)/emission from non-intervention fleet.   (B-21)

    Using the data from the benefits table of the Hurter taxicab report, the total emission can be computed. Line seven of this table shows a reduction of 2.1×10^5 grams per day HC, 25.5×10^5 grams per day CO and $.20 \times 10^5$ grams per day in NO_x resulting in percentage reduction in total CBD pollution of 4.96 percent HC, 5.45 percent CO and 0.62 percent NO_x. Therefore total emissions are:

$(2.1 \times 10^5)/.0496 = (2.1 \times 10^5)/(4.96 \times 10^{-2}) = .422 \times 10^7$, or 4.22

$\times 10^6$ grams per day HC,

$(2.55 \times 10^6)/(5.45 \times 10^{-2}) = 4.68 \times 10^7$ grams per day CO, and

$(2.10^4)/(6.2 \times 10^{-3}) = 3.23 \times 10^6$ grams per day NO_x.

Then the percentage reduction due to $S1$ over $S0$ is:

10^2 $(2.76 \times 10^5)/(4/22 \times 10^6) = 6.54$ percent reduction in HC,

$10^2 \, (3.03 \times 10^6)/(4.68 \times 10^7) = 6.47$ percent reduction in CO, and

$10^2 \, (2.12 \times 10^5)/(3.23 \times 10^6) = 6.56$ percent reduction in NO_x.

Considering the diversity in the assumptions employed and the roughness of the calculations, these estimates of the percentage reductions are surprisingly close to the earlier estimates. Since the second procedure is a little simpler to use, it is suggested that it be employed in future calculations. The weakest portion of the calculations remaining is the assumption that work-trips in the CBD generate 10 vehicle miles per trip and that 1.5 person trips are made on each vehicle trip.

Appendix C

The Effects of Demand on Air Quality Prediction: The Case of Mobile Source Pollution

T.E. Petzel
R.O. Zerbe

Most empirical studies examining the effects of the clear air acts amendments on mobile source pollution have failed to consider the elementary demand conditions surrounding the problem. The usual procedure has been to take an age and model distribution (often the last data year available) and assume it to be constant through time. The total registration of automobiles, and the corresponding miles driven, are extrapolated to the point in time under consideration. There the emission characteristics of the various automobiles are applied to this projected distribution, and an estimate of mobile source pollution is achieved.

The basic problem with this method is the omission of several important factors influencing this age and model distribution. It would be a good estimator if there were (1) no capital costs attached to automobile pollution control, (2) no corresponding maintenance costs—e.g., loss in fuel efficiency—and (3) the percentage age and model distribution of automobiles tended to be constant through time. Of course none of these conditions holds. Superficially, what one expects to happen with the present situation is a shift in demand away from the new low polluting (higher cost) automobiles toward older models that are more efficient and from larger cars with greater fuel penalties toward smaller cars. This would tend to reduce the effectiveness of air pollution control devices on newer cars, as the older, higher polluting vehicles are used more intensively than they would have been.

The analysis we have developed incorporates several of these parameters omitted in other projections. Figure C-1 is an outline of the analysis. The numbers in parenthesis are simply reference points for expositional purposes. Number 1, refers to components of analysis of new car markets, 2, to those of used car markets and their related scrapping rates and 3, to the elements of synthesis of the above in achieving a prediction of mobile source pollution

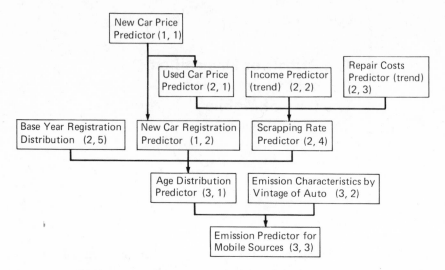

Figure C-1.   Flow of Analysis for Automobile Emission Predictions.

through time. The description of the analysis to follow will generally follow along these lines.

Two major shortcomings of this analysis must be noted. One is that no model is developed to predict changes in the size or engine power in response to price changes. The second shortcoming lies in the fact that the age distribution of automobiles in metropolitan areas is also a function of flow into and out of the metropolitan area in response to relative market conditions. As demand conditions change in one part of the nation, automobile movements in response to the change in demand conditions occur in other parts and thus the age distribution in any one metropolitan area may change in response to conditions elsewhere. Data could not be obtained sufficient to characterize these markets' interrelations. Thus, the prediction model is more accurate for the nation as a whole than for any particular metropolitan area.

NEW CAR PRICE PREDICTORS

To estimate the decline in demand for automobiles due to the provisions of the amendments to the Clean Air Act one must first estimate the increased costs resulting from the regulation. These fall into three types: (1) capital costs due to additional equipment necessary to control emissions, (2) added maintenance costs of this equipment and (3) operating costs due to any inefficiency these devices may impose. The maintenance and operating costs will be viewed as a discounted stream over the life of the car.

The way the standards are presently formulated, the major cost changes will be those given in Table C-1. It should be noted that in 1975 cataly-

Table C-1. Costs of Various Emission Standards for New Cars

	Additional Capital Costs	*Change in Lifetime Operating Costs*	*Change in Lifetime Maintenance Costs*
1973	$ 60	$106	$ 64
1975	$ 78	−$123	—
1976	$ 60	$176	$ 75
1977	$134	$239	$159

tic reactors will be installed, but it will be possible for much of the equipment presently found on automobiles to be removed. This will result in a net capital cost increase of $78, but it is anticipated that there will be an increase in fuel efficiency. In 1976 the equipment removed in 1975 will be reinstalled with a resulting large decline in fuel efficiency. The 1977 standards require a further reduction of NO_x. This will necessitate a further refinement in the catalytic reactor with accompanying increases in capital, operating and maintenance costs. Figure C-2 shows the growth path of discounted lifetime operating and maintenance costs. It also includes the expected increases due to the growth in driving. This rate of growth has been approximately two percent per year, which can be seen in the graph for years after 1971.

Since these costs for pollution control offer no capturable return to the persons owning these cars they are viewed as price increases with no corresponding quality change. In this study we have formulated a price series from this cost data and the historical trend of new car prices. This price series

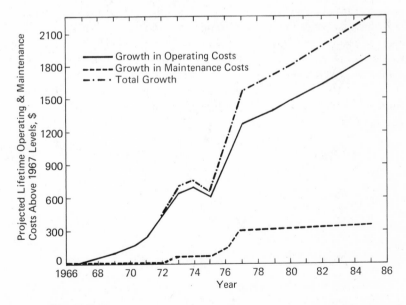

Figure C-2.

was then taken with the price elasticity of –.9 (from a study by Nerlove, which tends to be in agreement with other demand studies by Suits, Dyckman and Chow).[1, 2, 3, 4]

USED CAR PRICE PREDICTOR

A second factor to be analyzed is the interaction between new and used car prices. One expects that there is a link between the markets such that an autonomous increase in new car prices will result in an increase in used car prices. There is a substitution away from new cars towards used cars, shifting the demand for used cars outward. (Of course there is a corresponding negative income effect working in the opposite direction, but we assume it is of small magnitude.) If there were only one class of new cars and one group of substitutes (instead of the vector of substitutes we actually have) the analysis of the interaction would be a straightforward price theory exercise. However, there are many classes of used cars, and hence technically a matrix market interaction. In this study we shall postulate a simple model of this interaction that is intuitively appealing. It seems that a one year old car of similar class and styling is a better substitute for the services of a new car than the three year old trade-in. Similarly, the three year old vintage would appear a better substitute than a six year old, and so on. If we order ages we may hypothesize a linkage by "best substitutes." That is to say, an autonomous increase in new car prices will increase prices of one year old used cars, which in turn increases two year old used car prices, and this process continues throughout the vintages. This hypothesis contends that noncorresponding markets—e.g., markets for two and five year old cars—do not interact directly, but through the intervening vintages. This is borne out by the empirical analysis in which we found that market links were strongest between corresponding groups.

The equations that were tested ran prices of used cars (quarterly from 1957) on the prices of the vintage car immediately younger than the year in question.

$$P_{i(t)} = \alpha + \beta_i P_{(i-1)\,(t)} + \beta_2 P_{(i-1)\,(t-1)} + \beta_3 P_{(i-1)\,(t-2)} + \cdots \qquad \text{(C-1)}$$

where

P_i = price of automobile vintage i,

$P_{(i-1)}$ = price of automobile vintage $i - 1$, and

t = quarterly time subscript.

The independent variable was lagged to test the belief that equilibrium in these markets was not instantaneously achieved.

The used car prices by quarter were estimated by a sample of prices of standard sized automobiles in the *Detroit News* from 1957 to 1972, adjusted for yearly depreciation. No presently compiled data source contained price data by model year for a satisfactory time period. Prices were estimated for used cars of ages one to ten years and for the class of cars eleven years old and older.

It was found that best results were obtained when equations were in the form

$$P_{i(0)} = \alpha + \beta_1 P_{i-1(0)} + \beta_3 P_{i-1(-2)} . \tag{C-2}$$

This shows the price changes for one model year affect the next closest model year, with some significant effect occurring in two quarters immediately. The one quarter lag coefficient was less significant than that for the two quarters lag and was hence removed to reduce possible multilinearity. This was for interaction between markets for automobiles up to seven years; after that, equations with no lagged dependent variable appear best. Table C-2 presents a summary of results.

To test the link between noncorresponding markets, regressions were also run in various other forms:

$$P_{i(*)} = \alpha^1 + \beta_1^1 P_{(i-2)(*)} + \beta_2^1 P_{(i-2)(*-1)} + \beta_3^1 P_{(i-2)(*-2)} \tag{C-3}$$

Table C-2. Regression Summary

Dependent Variable P_i	Constant	Independent Variable		R^2
		$P_i - 1(0)$	$P_i - 1(2)$	
Used Car Price				
Age 1	−417.2	1.087**	.2052	.74
2	−180.0	.6205**	.2239*	.58
3	25.7	.4697**	.2644**	.60
4	−90.2	.5960**	.2460*	.52
5	−4.6	.4338**	.3016**	.61
6	52.9	.3548**	.2569**	.54
7	113.1	.3983**		.32
8	122.2	.2661**		.14
9	52.6	.4450**		.34
10	67.9	.3005**		.18
11	89.3	.0318		.02

**Significant at 99 percent confidence level.
*Significant at 95 percent confidence level.

and

$$P_{i\,(*)} = \alpha^{11} + \beta_1^{11} P_{(i-3)\,(*)} + \beta_2^{11} P_{(i-3)\,(*-1)} + \beta_3^{11} P_{(i-3)\,(*-2)} \,. \tag{C-4}$$

These were found to be inferior in all respects to the linkage equations between corresponding markets.

From the regression summary it may be seen that the explanatory power of equations decreases as the age of the automobile goes up. Simply, this may be seen as a reflection of the fact that two automobiles aged eight and nine respectively are probably much better substitutes than are a new and one year old auto. That is to say that there is probably considerably more noncorresponding market interaction for older cars, and hence the single linkage model loses some of its explanatory power.

It is now possible to insert our new car price predictions into the linkage equations and arrive at the matrix of used car prices (by age and time) that will be used in the following section.

SCRAPPING RATE PREDICTOR

The scrapping of automobiles may be viewed as a demand for a service like any other demand. As an automobile ceases to offer the particular stream of services desired by the owner it is either sold or it is scrapped. Variables which affect this decision include the price of the automobile in question, income and the cost of maintaining cars in running order. Data on national age distribution were obtained from *Automobile News Almanac* for the years 1957 through 1971. Regressions were run for each of the various groups aged one to fifteen years. The dependent variable in each equation was the percentage of automobiles of each age that was scrapped each year—for example, the percentage of six year old autos on July 1 which were not registered as seven year old autos the following July. The independent variables are: (1) used car prices for the appropriate vintage as determined in the preceding section, (2) deflated disposable income and (3) deflated Bureau of Labor Statistics Index of Automobile Repair. Results from selected regressions are seen in Table C-3. SR_i is the scrapping rate of cars aged i years. P_i is the market price of these cars i years of age. ADY is annual disposable income and $PFIX$ is repair cost index.

From the table it is obvious that the price of the automobile has little effect on scrapping until the automobile is rather old, in our case eight years of age. Prior to this the significance of the coefficients was quite small. This is probably what one should expect. Scrapping at an earlier age is probably due more to accidents or misuse than to the normal process of wearing out and disposal. Income likewise has its most significant effect on older cars. The price of repair costs, like income, seems significant for automobiles aged seven through ten years, but it enters with what appears to be the wrong sign;

Table C-3. Summary of Scrapping Rate Regressions

Dependent Variable SR_i	Constant	P_i	Independent Variables DY	PFIX	R^2
i = 1	-0.6275	0.001400*	-0.00130	0.4569	0.33
2	0.0573	-0.000052	0.00040	-0.0591	0.27
3	0.6940	-0.000180	0.00039	-0.0623	0.14
4	0.6468	-0.000280	0.00048	-0.0496	0.28
5	-0.4620	-0.000034	0.00022	0.0569	0.20
6	0.1376	-0.000160	0.00065	-0.1186	0.09
7	0.4869	0.000430	0.00195**	-0.5056**	0.47
8	1.0740	-0.001960*	0.00416**	-1.0900**	0.76
9	1.5180	-0.006520**	0.00612**	-1.5100**	0.80
10	1.8590	-0.020200*	0.00637**	-1.7010**	0.61
11	0.4360	-0.015050	0.00290	-0.1767	0.31
12	-0.1424	-0.031200*	-0.00850	0.6735	0.33
13	0.6424	-0.029100**	0.00100	-0.1692	0.35
14	1.1770	-0.021800*	0.00170	-0.7821	0.40
15	0.8550	-0.035300**	0.00110	-0.3329	0.51

**Significant at 99 percent level.
*Significant at 95 percent level.

as repair costs increase, scrapping rates for these cars decline! A previous study by Tolley and Wang ran annual tests over several decades instead of our 15 year study and found significant influence of scrapping rates for these ages with the normally expected sign. The explanation we offer for this discrepancy is that for 13 of the 15 years in our study the real price of repair did not vary more than two percent. Normally one would expect very little significance for a "constant" variable and this is the explanation we offer for these apparently spurious results. Removing the *PFIX* variable had the effect of increasing the significance of both the price and income variables, but reduced the R^2 for these four equations.

Tolley and Wang did not have a used car price variable in their study. They used instead new car prices for each of the scrapping rate ages and found very little of significance. This, of course, is not surprising in light of our findings in the section on used car prices. With the linkage in the markets as we found it there is both a lag in the response as the shift in new car prices filters down and a lack of completeness in the explanation of possible variation in the used car prices. Therefore, Tolley and Wang's new automobile price should not be expected to perform well when examining the marginal decision to scrap a nine year old auto. It would be expected to do well for younger autos but, as we have seen, the scrapping decision attached to these is not sensitive to any of our explanatory variables.

Tolley and Wang's findings also support the above finding that as the age of automobiles increases the scrapping decision becomes more sensitive to the listed variables. To a lesser extent, they support our finding that as cars become quite old the decision to scrap may be involuntary also due to the deterioration of the automobile beyond scope of normal repair (note declining R^2 after automobiles of age ten). We feel additional research would be fruitful in this area as Tolley and Wang's study had considerably less decline in R^2 with age.

AGE DISTRIBUTION PREDICTOR

If we now insert our predicted values of used car prices into our scrapping rate equations which have significant price coefficients, with the predicted trend variables for income and repair costs, we may predict these scrapping rates through time. Scrapping rates for autos less than eight years of age do not appear responsive to changes in our variables, so the mean values of these rates will be used. From the section on new car prices we have a prediction for new car sales through time. If we start with a base year distribution (1971), and with the predicted rate for providing the new stock of cars to the market, we may apply the predicted scrapping rates to get a predicted age distribution through time. Results of such a calculation are in Table C-4. The percentages of each automobile by age are given in Table C-5. The black line on

Table C-4.   Predicted Age Distribution

Model Year	1971	1972	1973	1974	1975	1976	1977	1978	1979	1980	1981	1982	1983	1984	1985
1985															10650
84														10442	10129
83													10237	9930	9890
82												10036	9735	9696	9647
81											9839	9544	9505	9458	9344
80										9646	9357	9319	9273	9161	8960
79									9457	9173	9137	9091	8982	8784	8442
78								9272	8994	8958	8913	8806	8612	8276	7689
77							9090	8817	8782	8738	8633	8443	8114	7538	6671
76						9421	9138	9102	9056	8448	8751	8409	7812	6922	5780
75					10022	9721	9682	9634	9518	9309	8946	8311	7363	6148	4956
74				9366	9085	9049	9003	8895	8700	8360	7767	6881	5753	4637	3538
73			9183	8908	8872	8827	8722	8529	8197	7615	6754	5647	4557	3467	2642
72		9467	9183	9146	9100	8991	8793	8450	7850	6963	5828	4703	3589	2727	2054
71	9729	9437	9399	9352	9240	9037	8684	8068	7148	5983	4834	3688	2803	2111	1558
70	8888	8852	8808	8702	8510	8177	7598	6739	5627	4547	3469	2636	1985	1465	1112
69	9280	9234	9123	8922	8574	7966	7058	5879	4739	3616	2748	2069	1527	1159	2932**
68	8802	8696	8505	8173	7593	6712	5591	4495	3430	2607	1963	1448	1099	2781*	
67	7772	7601	7304	6786	6006	5009	4027	3073	2335	1775	1336	986	2494*		
66	8313	7989	7422	6576	5498	4425	3377	2566	1432	1426	1082	2738*			
65	8171	7534	6705	5612	4523	3451	2623	1975	1458	1106	2799*				
64	6651	5787	4832	3962	3023	2298	1730	1277	969	2452*					
63	5624	4494	3379	2518	1913	1441	1063	807	2042*						
62	4274	3654	2798	2024	1524	1124	854	2159*							
61	2525	1880	1400	1034	763	579	1465*								
60	2034	1477	1120	797	605	1530*									
59	1183	897	628	451	1142*										
58	563	400	306	775*											
57	730	523	1346*												
56	580	1470*													
55	1804*														
Total	86934	88842	91441	93104	95993	97758	98498	99737	100234	101222	102156	102755	103440	104702	105994
Predicted total from regression		87879	90233	92588	94942	97297	99651	102010	104360	106710	109070	111420	113780	116130	118490
Percent Δ		+1.0	+1.3	+0.6	+1.1	+0.5	-1.2	-2.3	-4.1	-5.4	-6.8	-8.4	-10.0	-10.9	-11.8

Table C-5. Predicted Age Distribution Percentages

Age of Car	1971	1972	1973	1974	1975	1976	1977	1978	1979	1980	1981	1982	1983	1984	1985
1	11.1	10.6	10.0	10.1	10.4	9.6	9.2	9.3	9.4	9.5	9.6	9.8	9.9	10.0	10.1
2	10.2	10.6	10.0	9.6	9.5	9.9	9.3	8.8	9.0	9.0	9.2	9.3	9.4	9.5	9.6
3	10.6	10.0	10.3	9.8	9.2	9.2	9.8	9.1	8.7	8.8	8.9	9.1	9.2	9.3	9.3
4	10.1	10.4	9.6	10.0	9.5	9.0	9.1	9.6	9.0	8.6	8.7	8.8	8.9	9.0	9.1
5	8.9	9.8	10.0	9.3	9.6	9.2	8.8	8.9	9.5	8.8	8.4	8.6	8.7	8.7	8.8
6	9.5	8.6	9.3	9.6	8.8	9.2	8.9	8.5	8.7	9.2	8.6	8.2	8.3	8.4	8.4
7	9.3	9.0	8.0	8.8	8.9	8.4	8.8	8.5	8.2	8.2	8.8	8.2	7.8	7.9	8.0
8	7.6	8.5	8.1	7.3	7.9	8.1	7.7	8.1	7.8	7.5	7.6	8.1	7.6	7.2	7.2
9	6.5	6.5	7.3	7.1	6.3	6.8	7.2	6.7	7.1	6.9	6.6	6.7	7.1	6.6	6.3
10	4.9	5.0	5.3	6.1	5.7	5.1	5.7	5.9	5.6	5.9	5.7	5.5	5.6	5.9	5.4
11	2.9	3.5	3.7	4.3	4.7	4.5	4.1	4.5	4.7	4.5	4.7	4.6	4.4	4.4	4.7
12	2.3	2.1	3.0	2.7	3.1	3.5	3.4	3.1	3.4	3.6	3.4	3.6	3.5	3.3	3.3
13	1.4	1.7	1.5	2.2	2.0	2.3	2.7	2.6	2.3	2.8	2.7	2.6	2.7	2.6	2.5
14	0.6	1.0	1.2	1.1	1.6	1.5	1.8	2.0	1.9	1.8	1.9	2.0	1.9	2.0	1.9
15	0.8	0.4	0.7	0.8	0.8	1.1	1.1	1.3	1.4	1.4	1.3	1.4	1.5	1.4	1.5
16	0.7	0.6	0.3	0.5	0.6	0.6	0.9	0.8	1.0	1.1	1.1	0.9	1.1	1.1	1.0
>16	2.1	1.6	1.5	0.8	1.2	1.6	1.5	2.2	2.0	2.4	2.7	2.7	2.4	2.6	2.7

Table C-6. Aggregate Percentage of 1976-1977 Level Controlled
Cars in Total Registrations

	Prediction 1*	*Prediction 2***	$\Delta\% = \dfrac{P1 - P2}{P1}$
1976	11.1	9.6	13.5
1977	21.4	18.5	13.6
1978	32.0	27.2	15.0
1979	42.1	36.1	14.2
1980	51.0	44.7	12.4
1981	60.5	53.4	11.7
1982	69.8	62.0	11.2
1983	77.4	69.8	9.8
1984	83.9	76.5	8.8
1985	88.8	92.2	7.9

*Prediction 1 takes 1971 age distribution as constant and extrapolates through time.
**Prediction 2 is prediction based on Zerbe-Petzel model.

the second table divides autos between those which are controlled at the rigorous 1976-1977 standards and those which are not. Table C-6 presents an aggregate of the percentage of total automobile population controlled at this level using two prediction techniques. The first is the type used presently and simply extrapolates the 1971 distribution. The second is the result of our model. As one can see, as the less controlled automobiles drop out of the population the estimates converge. But the error in the first five or six years is not insignificant and could very well affect the expected return from these pollution control devices. Figure C-3 shows the expected total registration from our predictor versus a linear extrapolation of total registrations. The curves diverge as one moves past 1976 largely due to the decline in demand for new cars. In light of the increased costs of operation and purchase this result seems to be reasonable. In fact, with the present banter over increased costs due to the petroleum shortage we may be seeing a premature beginning of this effect. In the long run one would expect that there would be large substitution toward automobiles more economical to operate. This would reduce the trend depicted in Figure C-3, but some differential may still be expected.

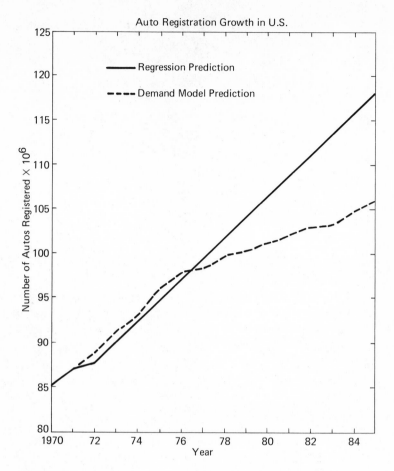

Figure C-3.

Appendix D

Emission Prediction and Control Strategy: Evaluation of Pollution from Transportation Sources

R.E. Wendell
J.E. Norco
K.G. Croke

To attain safe air quality levels each major urban area must develop a pollution control strategy. In the case of hydrocarbon, carbon monoxide and nitrogen oxide emissions, the determination of such a control strategy must include consideration of transportation pollution. In particular, alternatives such as parking restrictions, staggered work hours, promotion of mass transportation, commuter taxes and gasoline rationing should be considered from a short-term episode point of view as well as a long-range planning point of view. This paper presents a "total systems" approach in analyzing these alternatives. This approach is illustrated with data from an analysis of the Chicago area.

The "total systems" approach is based on the development of two models: a vehicle emissions model and an urban transportation model. The vehicle emissions model, which takes a new approach to vehicle emissions by distinguishing between "hot" and "cold" vehicle operation, is reviewed. Such an approach is important since by 1975 it is expected that new cars will emit 85 percent of their carbon monoxide and hydrocarbons during cold operation. The method of integration of the vehicle emissions model to an urban model is also discussed and illustrated with data from the Chicago Area Transportation Study. The combining of the models into an emission simulation technique and subsequent policy evaluation of urban emission reduction strategies is then illustrated. Among the results is an examination of the significance of mobile pollution sources and control strategies in the central business district of Chicago.

THE PROBLEM

With appropriate authority from the Clean Air Act, the federal Environmental Protection Agency promulgated air quality standards and required states to submit implementation plans to meet these standards. In this paper, we will consider only the problem of meeting the carbon monoxide, hydrocarbon and nitrogen oxide standards—e.g., those directly identifiable to vehicle emissions. To illustrate our approach, examples from the Chicago air quality region will be given.

As a guide to help the states analyze their problems, EPA suggested possible use of a rollback model [4: Appendix I]. We now compare this approach to our total systems approach.

Rollback

In the rollback approach the number of miles and the average speed for both the base year (1970) and the future target year (1975) by which federal air quality standards are to be met are determined. Then, based on given vehicle emission rates (expressed in grams of pollutants per vehicle mile), the total tons of CO, HC and NO_x can be calculated for the base and target years. Assuming that air quality determined from monitored air quality data for the base year in the region is proportional to total vehicular emissions, the air quality for the target year can be estimated by knowing the ratio of present to projected emissions.

If the estimated air quality for the target year is not smaller than EPA standards, then emission controls and/or transportation controls must be considered. Emission controls (e.g., retrofit, inspection-maintenance) give smaller emission rates but do not affect total vehicular mileage in the region while transportation controls tend to reduce traffic (e.g., miles traveled).

Total Systems Approach

Unfortunately, the above simplistic rollback approach ignores many important factors and provides little flexibility in analyzing control strategies. In particular, we cite the following limitations:

1. The spatial aspect of emission is ignored in that the approach implies only a regional total for emissions. In particular, the special problems and possible solutions of smaller areas (e.g., central business districts) are lumped into the regional problem.
2. The vehicle mix of the region is ignored in determining emission rates for vehicles. Since trucks emit more than cars and since newer cars emit less than older cars, the individual mix of each region (or of subregions within the region) should be considered. Chicago, for example, has a higher percentage of newer cars. As we will see, this has a significant effect on the analysis.
3. No distinction is made between hot and cold emissions of vehicles. Since 1975 cars are expected to emit 90 percent of their CO and 80 percent of their HC during the first two minutes of a typical trip, this aspect should become an important spatial consideration.
4. In failing to allow for the above considerations, the analysis of alterna-

tives is particularly inflexible. Any strategy based on certain classes of vehicles (e.g., inspection-maintenance, retrofit) is difficult to analyze. Further, a strategy that may be effective in limited subregion areas (e.g., CBDs) cannot be analyzed on a regional basis.

To alleviate the above problems our "total systems" approach was adopted. A prime consideration of the approach is a spatial breakdown of the region. Such a breakdown is accomplished by spatially subdividing the region into a number of grid squares.

For each square we obtain (from the Chicago Area Transportation Study) the corresponding transportation characteristics. Such characteristics include daily and peak hour mileage estimates, speed estimates and data on origins and destinations. Independently we estimate emission rates for vehicles in the region. In particular, we consider local registration data and truck percentages. Further, we permit consideration of the distinction between emissions from vehicles whose engines have attained normal operating temperatures and "start up" or "cold start" emissions.

By combining the appropriate emission rates with the transportation characteristics data for each grid square, we are able to estimate the emissions for each square. For the region, therefore, we generate an emissions map which gives a spatial view of emissions in the region. By simulating various control strategies, the changes in emissions that occur within each grid square of the region can easily be determined. In other words, the model has the flexibility to simulate emissions maps over the region for various control strategies. This procedure is illustrated in Figure D-1.

Such an approach as the above is not entirely new in analyzing air pollution strategies. The spatial aspect of emissions was considered by Ott, Clark and Ozolins in 1967.[7] Their work, however, did not include a vehicle

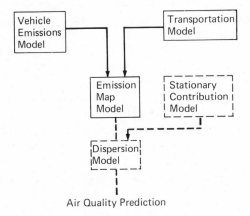

Air Quality Prediction

Figure D-1. The "Total Systems" Approach.

emissions model. Instead, the emission rates were gross estimates of grams per mile per vehicle and, in particular, no distinctions were made between trucks and automobiles, between hot and cold emissions and among model years. Thus, spatial accuracy as well as flexibility in control strategy evaluation was severely limited.

On the other hand, some unpublished work by EPA [2] includes an emissions model which is similar to the vehicle emissions model of this paper.[1] One main difference in the models is our distinction between hot and cold emissions.

Note that the total systems model can be viewed as a tool for simulating emissions maps. Such emissions maps could in turn be used to generate air quality maps via a dispersion model. One such dispersion model is given by Ott et al.[7]

VEHICLE EMISSIONS MODELS

The method of measuring vehicular emissions in order to estimate mobile source emission factors has undergone a series of changes. A good discussion of the history of various methods through the adoption of the 1972 Federal Driving Cycle is given by Pattison.[8] After the adoption of the federal cycle, the automotive manufacturers claimed that too much emphasis had been placed on the cold emissions.[5] The federal government subsequently revised the testing method to distinguish between hot and cold emissions, with the net result of deemphasizing the cold emissions.[6]

Unfortunately, the effectiveness of proposed emission control devices to reduce emissions from vehicles is not as effective on cold start emissions as on emissions from automobiles at normal running temperature. Thus, cold emissions from post–1974 cars will become increasingly significant. In particular, 90 percent of the CO and 80 percent of the HC will be emitted during the first two minutes. It is clear, therefore, that consideration of this effect will be important in the analysis of pollution emissions and their control. This is the motivation behind our vehicle emissions model.

Before reviewing the methodology of the cold start model (e.g., the methodology that considers the cold start effect), we first review the model developed by EPA. For simplicity, we will consider only the CO methodology. Except for minor differences in evaporation and crankcase hydrocarbon emission, analogous relationships exist for HC and NO_x.

The specific definitions of the classes that we use are as follows:

---

1. The vehicle emissions model is a generalization of this EPA model.

Class	*Type of Vehicle*
1	Passenger cars
2	Light Duty Trucks
3	Trucks (6000–10,000 lb, GVW)
4	Trucks (10,000–19,000 lb, GVW)
5	Trucks (over 19,000 lb, GVW).

For passenger cars, the average emission factor of a car in year y is:

$$E_{y_1} = \sum_{j=0}^{13} M_j \cdot D_j \cdot G_{y-j} \qquad (D-1)$$

where:

$$G_{y-j} \equiv C_s \cdot C_t \cdot g_{y-j} \qquad (D-2)$$

= corrected emission factor of $(y-j)$ year model car with age j,

$$M_j \equiv r_j \cdot m_j \Big/ \sum_{k=0}^{13} r_k \cdot m_k \qquad (D-3)$$

= fraction of vehicle miles that were driven by j year old passenger cars,

D_j = deterioration factor for cars of age j,

C_s = speed adjustment factor (0.766) which converts test cycle emissions at 10 mph to urban speed of 25 mph,

C_t = summer to annual conversion factor (1.085),

g_{y-j} = emission factor of $(y-j)$ year model car according to 1972 test cycle,

r_j = fraction of j year old cars in registration, and

m_j = average miles driven by a j year old car.

For ith class trucks ($i = 2, 3, 4, 5$) the average emission factor is:

$$E_{yi} = \sum_{j=0}^{15} M_j^t \cdot D_j^t \cdot C_i \cdot G_{y-j} \qquad (D-4)$$

where:

M_j^t = fraction of vehicle miles that were driven by j year old trucks,

D_j^t = deterioration factor for trucks, and

C_i = scaling factor based on truck weight.

Thus, the overall emission factor for year y is given by:

$$E_j = \sum_{i=1}^{5} P_i \cdot E_{yi} \tag{D-5}$$

where P_i is the fraction of vehicle miles driven by class i vehicles.

We can now see that Equations D-1 and D-4 were both based on the same logic that the average emission factor in year y, E_{yi}, is given by the weighted average of the corrected emission factor, G_{y-j}, over the fraction of vehicle miles driven by y year old vehicles and age deterioration factors (a class scaling factor for trucks). While the M_j's for passenger cars are determined from the registration data (as in Table D-1) according to Equation D-3, the M_j^t's for trucks are simply listed in Table D-2. Values for the other parameters are also given in Table D-2.

Using these values for the parameters the model yields the emission factors given in the first row of Table D-3. The second row of Table D-3

Table D-1. Registration Data

Age	j/r_j			
	Chicago	Cook County	Illinois	Federal
0	0.1126	0.1163	0.0963	0.109
1	0.1407	0.1444	0.1274	0.104
2	0.1265	0.1307	0.1208	0.100
3	0.1087	0.1124	0.1071	0.096
4	0.1068	0.1090	0.1099	0.091
5	0.1047	0.1074	0.0860	0.086
6	0.0840	0.0815	0.0864	0.080
7	0.0705	0.0671	0.0730	0.074
8	0.0558	0.0523	0.0580	0.066
9	0.0324	0.0296	0.0344	0.056
10	0.0256	0.0230	0.0285	0.045
11	0.0113	0.0101	0.0146	0.032
12	0.0047	0.0042	0.0062	0.017
13	0.0160	0.0149	0.0299	0.042

Table D-2.   Values of Parameters

y			g_y
1962–1967			110.0
1968–1969			63.2
1970–1971			47.0
1972–1974			39.0
1975–1980			4.7

	m_j	D_j	$D_j{}^t$	$M_j{}^t$
0	13200	1.063	1.075	0.100
1	12000	1.165	1.170	0.095
2	11000	1.210	1.215	0.090
3	9600	1.235	1.242	0.085
4	9400	1.252	1.275	0.080
5	8700	1.265	1.268	0.075
6	8600	1.275	1.280	0.070
7	8100	1.285	1.288	0.065
8	7300	1.292	1.288	0.060
9	7000	1.296	1.295	0.055
10	5700	1.299	1.300	0.050
11	4900	1.301	1.302	0.045
12	4300	1.302	1.303	0.040
13	4300	1.302	1.304	0.035
14	---	---	1.305	0.030
15	---	---	1.305	0.025

	C_i	P_i
1	----	0.830
2	1.0000	0.087
3	2.1555	0.025
4	2.8024	0.106
5	3.1715	0.042

corresponds to rural driving—e.g., average speed of 45 mph—and the numbers there follow from another correction factor.

The emission factors, given as the weighted averages in Table D-3, are based on a number of assumptions concerning the nature of vehicle emissions. Some of these assumptions—deterioration, speed correction factors, emission rates from various classes and increased use of newer model vehicles—appear to be reasonably independent of the particular region being considered.[2] Other assumptions, such as registration data and vehicle mix, may be directly dependent on a region or on that part of a region being considered. We will now review the significance to the emission rates of using regional data in Chicago instead of the federal data.

2. This ignores possible differences due to altitude, climate and local regulations and habits of maintenance.

Table D-3. **Motor Vehicle Emission Factors for 1975 Based on Federal Registration (grams per vehicle mile)**

	Class					
Emissions	*1*	*2*	*3*	*4*	*5*	*Weighted*[a]
Carbon Monoxide						
Urban	52.64	68.11	146.57	190.55	215.65	65.39
Rural	27.23	35.23	75.81	98.56	111.54	33.32
Hydrocarbons						
Evaporations	1.30	1.75	1.75	1.75	1.75	1.38
Crankcase	0.10	0.44	0.84	1.08	1.14	0.21
Exhausts						
Urban	5.64	7.66	14.56	18.62	19.82	6.84
Rural	3.38	4.58	8.71	11.14	11.85	4.09
Nitrogen Oxide						
Urban	6.48	7.02	9.75	20.04	27.24	7.70
Rural	6.66	7.21	10.02	20.60	27.99	7.91

[a]These weighted averages are approximately equal to the emission factors given in McGraw and Duprey.[6]

Registration Effects

Table D-1 compares the relative fractions of automobiles for each of the last 14 years in Chicago, Cook County, Illinois, and to the federal average. Note that Cook County has a higher percentage of newer cars than Chicago, which in turn has a higher percentage than Illinois, which in turn has a higher percentage than the federal average. Since newer cars will undergo significant reductions in emissions (due to requirements for manufacturers in the Clean Air Act), the effects of these reductions will have earlier and larger effects in Chicago. The vehicle emissions model's estimate of this effect is given in Table D-4 with a summary of different years given in Table D-5.

Note the higher percent reductions which occur because of the registration effect in Chicago and, in particular, the way the factors based on Chicago registration data give consistently higher reduction estimates. In 1975 carbon monoxide, for example, has approximately a four percent higher reduction estimate with respect to 1970 using the Chicago registration data than the federal prediction. With respect to 1975, the registration effect yields a six percent reduction for CO. Such an effect should not be ignored.

An example of the significance of this effect is an analysis of the effectiveness of retrofit. Based on retrofit effectiveness of 37 percent for CO for pre-1968 automobiles,[9] the model yields a six percent reduction in CO emissions for 1975 using Chicago registration data and a ten percent reduction using the federal registration data. In other words, the effectiveness of retrofit in Chicago is 40 percent less than federal estimates. It is also interesting that the emission rates for CO with retrofit under federal registration assumptions are similar to estimate of emissions under Chicago registration data and no retrofit.

Table D-4. Motor Vehicle Emission Factors for 1975 Based on Local Registration (grams per vehicle mile)

Emissions	*1*	*2*	*3*	*4*	*5*	*Weighted*
			Class			
Carbon Monoxide						
Urban	45.94	68.11	146.57	190.55	215.65	59.83
Rural	23.76	35.23	75.81	98.56	111.54	30.95
Hydrocarbons						
Evaporations	1.06	1.75	1.75	1.75	1.75	1.18
Crankcase	0.03	0.44	0.84	1.08	1.14	0.15
Exhausts						
Urban	4.75	7.66	14.56	18.62	19.82	6.10
Rural	2.84	4.58	8.71	11.14	11.86	3.65
Nitrogen Oxide						
Urban	6.21	7.02	9.75	20.04	27.24	7.48
Rural	6.39	7.21	10.02	20.60	27.99	7.68

Cold and Hot Emissions

Because of the nature of CO and HC emissions, special attention must be given, as discussed previously, to the period of operation immediately after starting the vehicle from a cold start—e.g., after the vehicle has not been operated within the previous eight hours. Although the official soak time for the 1972 federal test procedure is twelve hours, eight hours is sufficient for our purposes. Because of the catalytic control techniques, this effect in 1975 model year vehicles will be especially significant. This is illustrated in Figure D-2 with time being relative to the 1972 federal test procedure.

By approximating the emissions with a step function, as indicated in Figure D-2, we can distinguish between those extra emissions occurring at the origin (the area of *a b c d*) and the emissions rate that is proportional to miles

Table D-5. Urban Vehicle Emission Factors

	Federal			*Chicago*		
	CO	*HC*	*NO_x*	*CO*	*HC*	*NO_x*
1970						
g/mi	106.65	16.96	9.56	103.73	15.73	9.59
1975						
g/mi	65.38	8.63	7.70	59.83	7.43	7.48
(% reduc.)	(38.8)	(49.1)	(19.5)	(42.3)	(52.8)	(22.0)
1977						
g/mi	45.95	5.75	5.83	40.08	4.70	5.42
(% reduc.)	(57.0)	(66.1)	(39.0)	(61.4)	(70.1)	(48.5)
1980						
g/mi	25.03	3.05	3.65	21.56	2.41	3.13
(% reduc.)	(75.6)	(82.0)	(61.8)	(79.2)	(84.7)	(67.4)

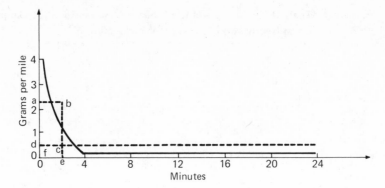

Figure D-2. 1975 Carbon Monoxide Emissions (based on the General Motors report to the Environmental Protection Agency [5]).

traveled (d grams per mile). Thus, vehicle emissions can be characterized by a cold start component (grams, g) occurring at an origin and a hot portion (grams per mile).

Letting f_y represent the fraction of emissions of carbon monoxide that occurs in the first two minutes of a "typical" trip, we use the following data drawn from Bowdith and Martens.[1]

y	f_y
1960–1967	0.45
1968–1970	0.55
1971	0.62
1972	0.69
1973	0.76
1974	0.83
1975–1980	0.90

Then we calculate the cold start componsent, S_y, for year y as

$$S_y = 7.5g_y \cdot f_y \; - \; \left\{ (7.5g_y)(1-f_y)\, \frac{1.5}{6.0} \right\}. \tag{D-6}$$

In Equation D-6, 7.5 is the number of miles of the 1972 cycle, 1.5 is the number of miles put on during the first two minutes and 6.0 is the number of miles put on after the first two minutes. Thus, $(7.5g_y)$ is the total number of grams of CO emitted over the cycle and $\{7.5g_y \cdot f_y\}$ is the number of grams emitted in the first two minutes. This corresponds to area $a\,b\,e\,f$ of Figure D-2. To find the area of *a b c d* we must subtract the area of *d c e f* which, in turn, is given by the second bracket in Equation D-6.

Expressing the rest of the emissions over the cycle as grams per mile, denoted as g'_y, we have the relationship

$$g'_y = 7,5g_y \, (1 - f_y)/6.0. \tag{D-7}$$

Letting g'_y replace the role of g_y in Equation D-2, Equations D-1, D-4 and D-5 give the grams per mile components of vehicle emissions. The resulting emission factors using Chicago registration data are given in Table D-6.

Comparing Table D-4 to Table D-6, we see that the grams per mile emissions of carbon monoxide in Table D-6 are one-half of those in Table D-4. On the other hand Table D-6 attributes over 200 grams of CO emissions to each cold start. Besides providing a different spatial distribution of emissions, the above effect is significant for analyzing control strategies. Consider, for example, a strategy involving a reduction of trip length—e.g., when people drive to mass transit parking instead of to work. An analysis of such a strategy using Table D-6 will indicate only about one-half the effectiveness of an analysis based on Table D-4 (e.g., instead of a ten percent reduction, the strategy will yield only a five percent reduction). One can easily imagine other cases where the distinction between hot and cold emissions will play a critical role. We will examine some such situations later in this paper.

Table D-6. Motor Vehicle Emission Factors for 1975 with Cold Start Component (grams per vehicle mile)

Emissions	Class					Weighted
	1	*2*	*3*	*4*	*5*	
Carbon Monoxide						
Urban	21.79	40.04	86.20	112.07	126.84	30.84
Rural	11.27	20.71	44.59	57.97	65.60	15.95
Hydrocarbons						
Evaporations	1.06	1.75	1.75	1.75	1.75	1.18
Crankcase	0.03	0.44	0.84	1.08	1.14	0.15
Exhausts						
Urban	2.99	5.87	11.17	14.28	15.21	4.14
Rural	1.79	3.51	6.68	8.54	9.10	2.47
Nitrogen Oxide						
Urban	6.21	7.02	9.75	20.64	27.24	7.48
Rural	6.39	7.21	10.02	20.60	27.99	7.68
	Cold Start Emissions (g)					
Carbon Monoxide	181.19	210.52	452.72	588.59	666.11	217.41
Hydrocarbons	15.73	20.20	38.43	49.12	52.29	18.76

URBAN TRANSPORTATION MODEL

From the previous discussion of vehicle emission factors, it is clear that certain kinds of transportation data are necessary to estimate emissions. In particular, we need to obtain the total number of cold starts and the number of miles traveled and corresponding speed data for each grid box in the region. Although such data are sometimes not readily available, we were fortunate in Chicago in that the Chicago Area Transportation Study (CATS) has a very large and detailed model of the region.

Working with CATS we were able to obtain the following daily and peak hour data for each grid box:

1. total arterial mileage and average arterial speed,
2. total freeway mileage and average freeway speed,
3. the number of work to home origins,*
4. the number of home to work origins,* and
5. other origins.*

Such data for the CBD are illustrated in Table D–7.

By considering the home-to-work origins as cold starts and the work-to-home origins as nine-tenths of a cold start, and by letting all other origins be one-half of a cold start, the total number of "equivalent" cold starts can be readily calculated for each grid box.

Besides providing a detailed data base, the CATS model has another distinct characteristic that adds a very important dimension to our approach. This dimension is the ability to simulate the transportation consequences of various transportation control strategies. For example, we evaluated the expected effects in the CBD if 50 percent of the trips from home outside the CBD to work in the CBD can be eliminated. Such a situation can, for example, be considered indicative of either mass transportation increases, traffic curtailment or some sort of parking regulations. In the next section we will consider the emission effects of such a strategy.

It should be mentioned that by combining vehicle count data on roads with the CATS data one can further estimate the effects of various highways in a region. This may be particularly significant when the vehicle mix on some roads is significantly different from other roads—e.g., a major truck route such as the Stevenson versus a major automobile route such as Lake Shore Drive. By using a line dispersion model the effects of a highway could be estimated. This is currently being researched by Argonne National Laboratory in conjunction with CATS.

---

*These three categories correspond to the CATS designation of long non-residential, long residential and short trips, respectively.

Table D-7. Transportation Inputs

Zones	Arterial Miles	Arterial Speed	Freeway Miles	Freeway Speed
60	18,100	12.3	-----	-----
61	53,100	9.0	-----	-----
62	60,100	14.0	-----	-----
63	74,700	11.3	56,500	41.1
64	132,600	6.3	-----	-----
65	113,300	9.4	-----	-----
68	54,200	12.8	100,000	40.6
69	104,300	6.2	-----	-----
70	116,600	14.7	-----	-----
71	64,700	7.9	-----	-----
72	24,900	11.7	59,000	41.4
73	92,500	21.2	-----	-----
Total	909,100		216,700	

	Work to Home Origins	Work Origins	Other
60	4,991	944	2,622
61	9,926	2,129	5,351
62	16,860	2,919	9,469
63	6,920	1,154	4,643
64	34,881	1,980	22,821
65	27,277	1,409	18,712
68	6,766	1,497	4,664
69	25,880	2,231	18,655
70	13,072	3,981	12,970
71	4,821	1,613	2,553
72	4,821	1,428	3,461
73	7,226	4,806	5,638

EMISSIONS MAP MODEL

The emissions map model simply determines the total number of grams of each pollutant emitted in each grid box. When one ignores the cold start phenomena, this consists simply of performing the calculations in Equation D-8 for each pollutant in each grid box.

Grams = (arterial miles) $\times$ (grams per mile) $\times$ (speed adjustment factor)

$\qquad$ + (freeway miles) $\times$ (grams per mile) $\times$ (speed adjustment factor).   (D-8)

Note that the arterial and freeway mileage numbers are for the particular grid box being considered. Further, the speed adjustment factor depends on the average speed on the corresponding type of road (e.g., arterial or freeway) in the grid box.[6]

When one considers the cold start phenomena, the calculation of emissions in each grid box is as given in Equation D-9.

Grams = (arterial miles) $\times$ (grams per mile) $\times$ (speed adjustment factor)

$\qquad$ + (freeway miles) $\times$ (grams per mile) $\times$ (speed adjustment factor)

$\qquad$ + (number of "equivalent" origins) $\times$ (grams per origin). $\qquad$ (D-9)

Unlike Equation D-8, D-9 has an extra term that corresponds to those emissions which result from the cold start phenomenon. The number of "equivalent" origins in this expression is the number of "equivalent" cold starts from the urban transportation model. Recall that the vehicle emission model gives the number of grams per origin as well as revised grams per mile factors to use in Equation D-9.

Table D-8 compares the emission differences of the different emission philosophies for CO and HC in the Chicago region. Again, the importance of using local registration data is evident. Note the difference between the cold start and the Chicago registration estimates. Except for HC in 1975, these estimated reductions on a regional basis are not significantly different. Since the cold start effect should average out over the region, this is not unexpected. For smaller areas, however, these differences may, indeed, be significant.

Table D-9 illustrates these differences for the CBD. It also illustrates the emissions of CO that would occur under a 50 percent traffic curtailment for both cases. Without cold start we see that the emission reduction in the CBD is 25 percent, whereas, with cold start the reduction is 33 percent.[3] This illustrates the importance of this "total systems" approach in analyzing such transportation control alternatives. In particular, just as cold start alternatives tend to make transportation controls more attractive, they could also make emission controls less attractive. Thus, determination of the most cost-effective strategy could directly depend on consideration of the cold start phenomena.

In conclusion, note that the approach that we presented is a general method for analyzing the many possible strategies for transportation pollution control. Furthermore, it is specific enough to allow for consideration of the important characteristics of the particular region being considered. Although the approach was illustrated with respect to the Chicago region, it can certainly be applied to any transportation pollution situation.

Finally, note that only a sample of strategy evaluations were made for Chicago. Analysis of inspection-maintenance strategies as well as various

3. These reduction estimates are based on preliminary calculations from the model.

Table D-8. Chicago Region Comparative Reductions

	HC			CO		
	Federal	*Chicago Region*	*Cold Start*	*Federal*	*Chicago Region*	*Cold Start*
1970						
Grams	$12,866 \times 10^5$	$11,158 \times 10^5$	$11,780 \times 10^5$	$83,926 \times 10^5$	$74,572 \times 10^5$	$68,175 \times 10^5$
1975						
Grams	$6,999 \times 10^5$	$5,290 \times 10^5$	$6,076 \times 10^5$	$57,074 \times 10^5$	$43,018 \times 10^5$	$38,169 \times 10^5$
(Percent reduction)[a]	(45.7)	(52.6)	(48.4)	(32.0)	(42.3)	(44.0)
1977						
Grams	— —	$3,195 \times 10^5$	$3,030 \times 10^5$	— —	$27,183 \times 10^5$	$23,967 \times 10^5$
(Percent reduction)[a]		(71.4)	(74.3)		(63.5)	(64.8)
1980						
Grams	— —	$1,558 \times 10^5$	$1,322 \times 10^5$	— —	$13,683 \times 10^5$	$11,890 \times 10^5$
(Percent reduction)[a]		(86.0)	(88.8)		(81.7)	(82.6)

[a]Based on 1970 emissions.

Table D-9.   1975 Central Business District Emissions

Zone	NO_x	HC		Before Curtailment		After Curtailment	
		Non-cold Start	Cold Start	Non-cold Start	Cold Start	Non-cold Start	Cold Start
60	1,124.0	1,559.5	2,688.7	15,086.8	19,379.7	12,998.7	13,534.3
61	3,294.4	4,925.0	6,641.5	48,742.3	48,009.1	30,783.9	29,540.9
62	3,732.2	4,856.9	8,828.8	45,994.7	63,177.1	31,938.4	40,835.9
63	8,246.1	8,930.8	8,502.9	79,237.3	55,164.9	65,955.6	39,990.8
64	8,234.5	12,310.2	19,131.0	121,832.8	138,930.0	108,037.2	97,422.2
65	7,035.9	10,518.5	15,631.8	104,100.0	113,362.1	60,714.2	66,876.7
68	9,794.2	8,673.2	8,489.3	69,746.8	51,052.9	57,952.4	37,557.8
69	7,668.9	10,419.6	15,496.5	100,346.1	110,740.3	50,893.8	63,110.5
70	7,240.9	9,197.9	11,645.1	86,361.9	81,242.6	82,024.1	63,574.3
71	4,817.9	6,006.6	5,683.8	59,446.3	40,476.7	38,522.9	31,713.0
72	5,348.4	4,587.1	5,045.4	36,256.5	40,780.0	31,094.7	23,396.8
73	5,741.1	5,710.2	7,389.4	48,169.7	48,445.1	36,140.8	34,668.8
Total	72,278.5	87,695.5	115,174.2	815,321.2	810,760.5	607,056.7	542,222.0

combinations of various strategies were not given. Also, analysis of peak rush hour effects is not included. The model can, of course, easily evaluate any of these possibilities. Furthermore, it can analyze these strategies for any year and, in particular, can evaluate the increasingly important cold start phenomena for post–1975 years.

Retrofit of In-use Vehicles

R.O. Zerbe
J. Meil
J. Cavallo

RETROFIT PROGRAM COSTS

There are three sources of cost associated with any retrofit program for automobiles. The first of these costs are those for purchase and installation, resulting from the manufacture of the device and the labor and materials needed to attach the device to the automobile. We call these capital costs. The second cost group is the operating costs, which consist of additional fuel costs incurred by operating the car with the attached device, compared to operation of the same car without the device. With a few emission control devices there is a net fuel saving when they are used, and the calculations are adjusted appropriately for the fuel saving in these cases. The third group of costs is maintenance costs, which consist of those repair costs directly associated with the continued effective operation of the device itself and the additional repair costs incurred by the other parts of the automobile as a result of the operation of the device. The devices to be evaluated as retrofit devices are the following:

1. Positive Crankcase Ventilation System (PCV). This device controls emissions from the crankcase and completely eliminates them. The hardware for this device consists of a simple valve and hoses, so capital and installation costs run to $5 or less for factory installation. The PCV system has no effect on fuel consumption and the only maintenance requirements for it are annual valve replacements at a cost of about $5. The PCV system was installed as standard equipment for automobiles in 1968. Therefore, the PCV system is applicable only to those model-years previous to and including 1968.

2. The Smog-Package Tuneup (SMOG). This is not really a device, but a standard tuneup which adjusts the air-fuel ratio and idling in order to reduce exhaust emissions. The tuneup would be done once a year, at an annual cost of $30. It would add nothing to the costs of operating a car and would eliminate the need for normal tuneup maintenance, saving the motorist

$10 per year in maintenance costs. Since 1968 model cars are equivalently
adjusted when they come off the assembly line, the smog-package tuneup
is effective only on 1967 and prior year cars.

3. Evaporation Control (EC). This device does not affect crankcase
or exhaust emissions, but does almost completely control the emissions from
the fuel system and fuel tank. It consists of a special tank, fuel lines and a
modified carburetor. Its main disadvantage is that it is quite expensive, since
the installation requires removal of the old fuel system and expenses for this
can run to$150. Maintenance is simple, averaging only $9 per year. Since the
evaporation control system prevents the loss of fuel to the atmosphere, the
motorist saves about $3 per year in fuel expenses—that is, operating cost in
this instance is negative. The modified fuel tank of this system became standard
equipment for cars in 1971, and therefore the evaporation control system is
applicable as a retrofit device for cars in 1970 and previous model-years.

4. Spark-Retard (SR). This device, as with the smog-package tuneup,
involves little in the way of extra parts and consists mainly of minor adjustments in an uncontrolled automobile. The procedure is to tune the engine to
the lowest emission levels while restricting the vacuum advance in some driving
modes. Maintenance is important for the successful operation of this method,
and fuel consumption increases by one to three percent. Therefore, costs of
purchase and installation are $35, while annual operating costs are $7.50 and
maintenance costs are $25. It can be applied successfully to automobile model-
years 1967 and previouş

5. The American Pollution Control System (APCS). This system is
an attempt by the American Pollution Control Corporation to combine two basic
approaches to emission control, the spark-retard system and the exhaust recycle
system, in a single package. It offers a greater degree of emission control at a
slightly lower cost than the two devices considered separately. The capital cost
for this device is $50 and the annual maintenance costs are $12. There are no
additional operating costs incurred from the use of this device, and it is applicable to pre–1968 automobiles.

6. The DuPont Flame Afterburner (DFA). This is designed to
drastically reduce HC and CO emissions by completing the burning of the exhaust gases through the use of a sustained flame. The hardware required for
this device is quite extensive, as reflected in the purchase and installation cost
of $200. The maintenance cost for the device is rather low, considering its
complexity, at $20 per annum, but this estimate is on the low side since it
includes only the maintenance costs required by the device itself and does not
include the possible damage to other parts of the car resulting from the intense
heat radiation. In order to operate most efficiently, it must work with a lower
air-fuel ratio and, therefore, gas mileage will probably decline in the neighbor-
hood of ten percent resulting in average annual operating costs of $32. It
will be applicable to all automobiles except 1975 vehicles, which will be controlled to equivalent levels.

7. Catalytic Reactor (CR). This is the emission control device that Detroit automakers were depending upon to enable their 1975 models to meet the strict standards originally proposed for that year. The hardware involved consists mainly of a converter chamber located between the exhaust manifold and the muffler, where a platinum or platinum-activated base metal catalyst in the form of a plate or pellets serves to promote the chemical conversion of HC and CO to water and carbon dioxide. Estimates of the cost of the catalytic reactor system range from $125 to as high as $175.

The cost estimates here are the products of a series of simplifying assumptions which are necessary in light of uncertainties about the devices and the vehicle population to be equipped. The most difficult problem is that retrofitting a V-8 is a much more difficult problem than retrofitting a six cylinder automobile. Under certain manufacturer's plans (such as Gould, Inc.) two converters will be used for the V-8, while only one converter will be used for the six cylinder car. At the very least, the catalytic converter for a V-8 will have to be a much more effective, and therefore more expensive, device to produce the same reduction levels as a device used on a six cylinder engine.

Another difficulty is that the use of the air pump varies widely among vehicle manufacturers and models. As a general rule, a higher percentage of GM cars have the air pump compared with the other two leading manufacturers. But policies among the different makes vary widely. For example, 1965 through 1968 Cadillaces were equipped with air pumps, but for 1969 model-year vehicles air pumps were dropped for the Cadillac line.

Yet another problem is that estimates of cost on mass production and mass installation of the catalytic muffler vary depending on how optimistic or pessimistic the engineer you are asking is. Optimistic estimates for the mass production and installation cost of the catalytic reactor can run as low as $35 per automobile on the average (not including air pump installation). The pessimistic estimates, once again for the catalytic reactor alone without air pump installation, run as high as $180. The best estimates available to us at the present time run from a range of $65 for a six cylinder car already equipped with an air pump, to almost $200 for a V-8 requiring air pump installation.

In light of the information above, we took the cost estimates of the Environmental Protection Agency and adjusted them. First, we retained their estimates of $85 for the reactor device and $58 for the air pump, for we believed they accurately represented the weighted average of equipping the automobile population. Then we made the assumption that all cars prior to 1968 needed to be equipped with air pumps, 50 percent of 1968-1972 vehicles needed air pumps and all post-1972 were equipped by the manufacturer. Therefore, our final estimate of retrofit cost, on the average, was $143 for pre-1968 cars, $113, for vehicle years 1968 through 1972 and $85 for model-years 1973 and after.

The principal maintenance requirement of the catalytic reactor is the replacement of the catalytic agent after every 25,000 vehicle miles driven. Estimates for the cost of replacement range from $25 to $105 per 25,000 miles. For our calculations we used an intermediate figure, $37.50 per 25,000 miles, which includes not only the catalyst replacement but also a $3 maintenance charge per 10,000 miles for cleaning the air pump.

The catalytic reactor increases fuel costs in two ways. First, successful operation requires a low air-fuel ratio, thereby imposing a one to five percent decrease in gas mileage. Second, the catalytic converter needs nonleaded gas to prevent the chemical degradation of the active catalyst material, and that adds one to two cents extra to the cost of each gallon of gasoline purchased. In our calculations we have assumed that there is a low fuel penalty in the use of a catalytic reactor, and therefore the operating cost figure we used was $18 per 10,000 miles.

8. Exhaust Gas Recycling (EGR). This system returns a portion of the exhaust gases through the carburetor to the combustion chamber. By altering the composition of the air-fuel mixture in this way a sizable reduction of NO_x emissions can be obtained. It is applicable in conception to cars which do not have any hardware for NO_x control, which would include all pre-1972 American cars. Purchase and installation cost would be on the order of $50. Operating costs would be unaffected and maintenance for the device would cost about $6 annually due to its simple operation.

9. Speed Controlled Exhaust. If the same idea is used with some refinements—that is, if the amount of exhaust gas recirculated into the system is made dependent upon the speed of the auto—we have what is known as the "speed controlled exhaust gas recirculation system." With this device, a speed control allows 15 percent of the exhaust gas to be recycled to the intake manifold whenever vehicle speed exceeds 26 mph, and shuts off the circulating system when speed is less than 12 mph. Due to the increased complexity of this system, the capital costs for this device are higher than for the simpler EGR system, coming to about $90. Maintenance costs are also fairly high, again due to the complexity of the device. Cleaning the exhaust gas recirculation valve and the solenoid vacuum valve filter comes to around $12 per 10,000 miles. However, the device is expected to contribute to a large saving in fuel due to the speed control feature. Tests run by the Environmental Protection Agency showed a seven percent fuel savings figure, although the statistical significance of the figure was not known. For our calculations we used an operating cost figure of $42 per 10,000 miles driven.

10. Dual Catalytic Reactor (CDR). This is an elaboration of the catalytic reactor discussed earlier. The difference between the two is that an extra type of catalyst is added to the above system in order to treat nitrogen oxide emissions which the single catalyst is not designed to control.

The additional hardware of the system consists of two NO_x converters placed slightly ahead of the single HC-CO catalyst converter in the automobile's exhaust escape system. The purchase and installation cost of the two NO_x reactors is $78. Therefore, 1975 models can be equipped with the dual catalytic reactor merely for the cost of the NO_x reactors, $78. 1968–1974 model-years can have the dual catalyst system at $143, and pre–1968 vehicles, which need an air pump in addition to the NO_x and HC-CO reactors, can have it at a total cost of $228.

An engine equipped with a dual catalytic reactor is very expensive to operate. Compared with an uncontrolled vehicle, the effective operation of a car with the dual catalyst system requires at least 25 percent more fuel; therefore, we have assessed operating costs at $120 per 10,000 miles driven. Maintenance costs for the system are also fairly high, at an average of $25 per 10,000 miles.

11. Air Bleed to Intake Manifold (AMIM). This system consists of an air valve that enables the air-fuel ratio to be increased by metering additional air to the intake manifold in accordance with the intake manifold vacuum. The costs of the hardware and the installation are $60. The fuel consumption effects measured in the federal tests showed a four percent improvement, which would result in operating savings of about $24 per 10,000 miles. Maintenance costs for this system are reasonably low due to the simplicity of the device, coming to approximately $6.30 per 10,000 miles.

12. Ignition Timing Modification (ITM). This system consists of an ignition control assembly attached to the fender wall. It includes a solenoid-operated valve which connects or disconnects the distributor vacuum advance, an ignition circuit which regulates the distributor point signal to a retarded condition at vehicle speeds below 35 mph, and a sequencing circuit and switch which sense vehicle speed and control the regulation provided by the first two items. The installation cost for this package is $45. Operating costs are about $6 per 10,000 miles driven and the cost of maintenance, including replacement for failure of the device, would be $12.50 per 10,000 miles driven. The device would be applicable to pre–1968 autos.

13. Natural Gas Conversion. This system for the control of automobile emissions, which is still in the planning stages, is the conversion of automobiles to run on natural gas or liquid petroleum gas. Unfortunately, figures on maintenance and reliability are not available, but the estimated engine conversion costs are $350.

14. Alter Gas Conversion. An idea in a similar vein is to alter the composition of the gasoline itself through adjustments in the refining process. There would be no capital costs imposed on the owner directly. However, the costs to refiners would be about $0.00169 per vehicle mile driven.

15. Used Car Kit. This simple device is marketed by General Motors for about $8, and with installation the total cost is no more than $40. There is no maintenance cost, and the operating cost resulting from the two to three percent reduction in gasoline mileage is about $13.50 per 10,000 miles driven.

RETROFIT PROGRAM BENEFITS

Aside from the fuel savings that result from the use of a few of the pollution control devices mentioned above, the principal benefit obtained from a retrofit program is, of course, emission reduction. Control technology has been concerned with three kinds of chemicals in auto emissions that pollute the atmosphere: hydrocarbons (HC), carbon monoxide (CO) and nitrogen oxides (NO_x). The problem of controlling these pollutants is compounded by the fact that quite frequently the methods used to control HC and CO are not only different from those used to control NO_x, but they sometimes work against each other. For example, the use of an exhaust gas recycling system to control NO_x emissions requires an enrichment of the air-fuel ratio to compensate for the decreased flame speed, but then the higher engine temperature causes CO and HC emissions to rise. Therefore, engineers are often faced with a trade-off between the degree to which they wish to control NO_x as opposed to HC and CO.

The emissions reduction figure for each device which follows is given in terms of a grams per mile change over an uncontrolled vehicle. The standard for an uncontrolled vehicle is derived from the federal test procedure (seven mode cycle). The measurements are: crankcase HC emissions 3.15 grams per mile; fuel tank HC emissions 2.77 grams per mile; exhaust HC emissions 10.20 grams per mile; exhaust CO emissions 76.9 grams per mile; and exhaust NO_x emissions 4.0 grams per mile.

The positive crankcase ventilation system has no effect on exhaust or fuel tank emissions but does control emissions from the crankcase with 100 percent effectiveness. The net HC reduction of the PCV system is 3.15 grams per mile.

The smog-package tuneup decreases hydrocarbon emissions by 24 percent or by 2.45 grams per mile. Carbon monoxide emissions are decreased by 15 percent to 65.4 grams per mile, a net reduction of 11.5 grams per mile. The adjustment of the air-fuel mix causes NO_x emissions to rise by 10 percent to 4.4 grams per mile, and this is an increase of 0.4 grams per mile over an uncontrolled vehicle.

The evaporation control device has no effect on emissions other than those from the fuel tank. Hydrocarbon emissions were reduced by 2.77 grams per mile, a factor of 95 percent, to a level of 0.14 grams per mile.

The American Pollution Control System combines two different approaches in the same package—the spark-retard system and the exhaust recycle—and thereby produces significant reductions in all three pollutants. Hydrocarbons were reduced by 3.06 grams per mile, or 30 percent. Carbon monoxide emissions were reduced by 35 percent, or 26.9 grams per mile. Nitrogen oxide emissions were reduced by 30 percent, from 4.0 grams per mile to 2.8 grams per mile.

The flame afterburner by itself controls HC and CO emissions effectively, but in combination with an exhaust recycling system it can also reduce NO_x emissions. The flame afterburner reduces HC emissions by 95 percent, from 10.20 grams per mile to 0.51 grams per mile, a reduction of 9.69 grams per mile. Carbon monoxide would be reduced by 95 percent, from 76.9 grams per mile to 3.85 grams per mile. Nitrogen oxide emissions would be reduced by 80 percent to 0.8 grams per mile.

The catalytic converter presents some very interesting problems. Since the single catalytic reactor is aimed primarily at controlling HC and CO emissions, Downing and Stoddard assumed that NO_x would be uncontrolled. However, the Environmental Protection Agency's report on vehicle control strategies gave the results of a test which found that the catalytic reactor was less effective in controlling HC and CO than Downing and Stoddard reported, but also reduced NO_x emissions by 40 percent. Therefore, the percent reduction figures we used for the single catalytic converter for HC, CO and NO_x were 95, 94 and 40 percent in that order. Not to be overlooked are the benefits gained from the fact that the converter must run on low lead fuel, which reduces the lead contamination of the atmosphere.

For the simple exhaust recycle system we assumed that only NO_x would be affected by the operation of the device. Nitrogen oxide reductions amounted to 2.0 grams per mile, a 50 percent cut. For the speed controlled exhaust gas recirculation system, NO_x was reduced by approximately the same amount, a 48 percent reduction to 2.08 grams per mile. However, test results also showed a 12 percent reduction in hydrocarbons and a 31 percent reduction in carbon monoxide, a total reduction of 1.94 and 35.4 grams per mile respectively.

The dual catalytic reactor system effectively controls all three of the major pollutants. Hydrocarbons are reduced by 95 percent from 10.2 grams per mile to 0.51 grams per mile. Carbon monoxide emissions are reduced by 90 percent, to 7.69 grams per mile. NO_x emissions are reduced by 90 percent from 4.0 grams per mile to 0.4 grams per mile. Once again, due to the operation of the car on low lead gasoline, lead emissions are also reduced.

Test results showed that the air bleed to intake manifold system reduces HC and CO but causes a net increase in the NO_x emissions. Hydrocarbon levels were reduced to 8.06 grams per mile, for a reduction of 21 percent over an uncontrolled vehicle. Carbon monoxide was reduced by 50 percent to 38.4 grams per mile, and nitrogen oxide levels increased by five percent, or from 4.0 to 4.2 grams per mile. However, it should be noted that EPA found this figure to be not significantly different from zero.

Ignition timing modification with lean idle adjustment successfully removed all three pollutants from the auto exhausts. Hydrocarbons were reduced by 19 percent to 8.26 grams per mile, a reduction of 1.94 grams per mile. Carbon monoxide emissions were reduced 37 percent from 4.0 grams per mile to 2.52 grams per mile.

The conversion of engine fuel from gasoline to natural gas or liquid petroleum gas causes significant reduction in emissions from the crankcase, the fuel tank and the exhaust. The converted system would have no crankcase hydrocarbons and no evaporation from the fuel tank, and there would be no lead pollution from the fuels, which would not contain lead. There would also be reductions in the hydrocarbon, carbon monoxide and nitrogen oxide levels of the exhaust of 94, 91 and 85 percent respectively.

The modification of gasoline composition has no effect on any emissions except for those from the fuel tank. The altered gasoline would reduce evaporated hydrocarbons by 60 percent to 1.11 grams per mile, from the uncontrolled level of 2.77 grams per mile.

The used car kit reduced all three pollutants from the automobile exhaust. Hydrocarbon levels were reduced by 50 percent to 5.1 grams per mile. Carbon monoxide levels were reduced by 23.1 grams per mile, a 30 percent reduction, while nitrogen oxides were also reduced 30 percent, from 4.0 grams per mile to 2.8 grams per mile.

In our calculations, we made the simplifying assumption that the effects of pollution control devices were cumulative in effect—that is, if a certain device reduces an uncontrolled vehicle's emissions by 30 percent, it will have a 30 percent reduction effect on the emissions of a vehicle which has some controls for emissions as part of its standard equipment. The Downing and Stoddard report [6] shows that this assumption is acceptable as long as only two or three different devices or methods are involved, and as long as there is not a great gap in the technological sophistication of the devices.

In order to obtain an unambiguous measure of effect, the three pollutants were weighted by factors relating to their relative damages (Appendix A) and summed. The costs and effects are determined for all of the years between 1975 and 1985 and discounted to present value at a six percent rate. The cost-effectiveness ratio then represents the ratio of these two figures.

Notes

CHAPTER TWO
FEDERAL POLICY FOR CONTROL
OF TRANSPORTATION EMISSIONS

1. Avaichou, Y.; Zerbe, R.; Portincaso, J.; and "A Statistical Analysis of Chicago CBD Parking: Unpublished Report to the University of Chicago-Argonne Joint Environmental Project, Chicago, 1973.
2. Ayres, Robert V. "Economic Impact of Mass Production of Alternative Low Emissions Automobile Power Systems." Air Pollution Control Association Conference, Chicago, 1973.
3. *Control Strategies for In-Use Vehicles.* Washington, D.C.: U.S. Environmental Protection Agency, November 1972.
4. *Control Techniques for Carbon Monoxide, Nitrogen Oxide, and Hydrocarbon Emissions From Mobile Sources* (AP66) Washington, D.C.: U.S. Department of Health, Education, and Welfare, 1970.
5. Conversation with John Moran, Environmental Protection Agency, 1974.
6. Creighton, R. *Urban Transportation Planning.* University of Illinois, Chicago, 1970.
7. *Cumulative Regulatory Effects on the Cost of Automobile Transportation* (RECAT), Final Report. Office of Science and Technology. Washington, D.C., 1972.
8. Dewees, D.N. *Economic Analysis of Automobile Pollution Control Policies.* Toronto: University of Toronto, January 1973.
9. "The Impact of Urban Transportation Investment on Land Value." University of Toronto, York University, Joint Program in Transportation, Research Report No. 11, 1973.
10. Downing, P. and Stoddard, L. *Economics of Air Pollution Control for Used Cars,* Riverside: University of California, 1973.
11. Horowitz, J. "Retrofit for Reducing Automobile Emissions: Effectiveness and Cost." *Journal of the Air Pollution Control Association* (May 1973) 23: 395.

173

12. Kircher, P.S. and Armstrong, P.P. *An Interim Report on Motor Vehicle Emissions Estimation.* Washington, D.C.: U.S. Environmental Protection Agency, Office of Air and Water Programs, Office of Air Quality Planning and Standards, May 1973.

13. Patterson, D.J. and Henein, N.A. *Emissions From Combustion Engines and Their Control.* Ann Arbor, Ann Arbor Science, 1972.

14. Reed, T.B. and Lerner, R.M. "Methanol: A Versatile Fuel for Immediate Use." *Science* (December 1973) 182: 1299.

15. *Report by the Committee on Motor Vehicle Emissions.* Washington, D.C.: National Academy of Sciences, February 12, 1973.

16. Strate, H.E."Annual Miles of Automobile Travel," Nationwide Personal Transportation Study, Report No. 2. Federal Highway Administration, Washington, D.C.: U.S. Dept. of Transportation, Office of Highway Planning, April 1972.

17. Wendell, R.E.; Norco, J.E.; and Croke, K.G. "Evaluation of Pollution from Transportation Systems." *Journal of the Air Pollution Control Association* (February 1973) Vol. 23, no. 2.

18. Zerbe, R.O. "Optimal Environmental Jurisdictions." *Ecology Law Quarterly,* September 1974.

CHAPTER THREE
EMISSION REDUCTION STRATEGIES

1. "Advantages of Key Mode Emission Testing Over Idle." Communication from Clayton Manufacturing Co., 1974.

2. Avichai, Y.; Zerbe, R.O.; and Portincaso, J. "A Statistical Analysis of Chicago CBD Parking." Report to Argonne-University of Chicago Joint Environmental Project.

3. "Bonus Features of Underload Modal Testing with Diagnostic Information." Clayton Manufacturing Co., August 1973.

4. Carlson, R.R.; Huls, T.A.; Kuhrts, S.G.; and Wilson, G.M. "Effectiveness of Short Emission Inspection Tests in Reducing Emissions Through Maintenance." Olson Laboratories Inc., 1974.

5. Conversation with Bob Latovich, Chicago Department of Environmental Control, August 22, 1973.

6. Conversation with Lee Tinkam, Clayton Manufacturing Company, August 1973.

7. Conversation with Archimedes Riviera, State of New York Pollution Control Agency, September 1973.

8. *Control Strategies for In-Use Vehicles.* Washington, D.C.: U.S. Environmental Protection Agency, November 1972.

9. *The Economic Effectiveness of Reducing Vehicle Exhaust Emissions,* vol. 2. San Bernardino, California, NTIS PB 209 952, TRW Systems Group, 1972.

10. *Evaluating Transportation Controls to Reduce Motor Vehicle Emissions in Major Metropolitan Areas.* Office of Air Programs Publication No. APTD-1364. Washington, D.C.: U.S. Environmental Protection Agency, November 1972.

11. Fijal, A. *Resurvey of Private Auto Travel in the Chicago CBD*. Chicago: Chicago Area Transportation Study, November 1, 1972.

12. Guttman, J. *The Value of Travel Time*. Chicago: University of Chicago, Urban Economics Report, 1974.

13. *Highway Capacity Manual*. Washington, D.C.: Highway Research Board, 1965.

14. Hurter, A.P., Jr. *Report on Proposal to Use Gaseous Fuels in Chicago Taxicab Fleet*. Evanston, Ill., Report to University of Chicago, Argonne Joint Environmental Project, August 1973.

15. Kitch, E.W.; Isaacson, M.; and Kasper, D. "The Regulation of Taxicabs in Chicago," *Journal of Law and Economics* (October 1971) 14: 285–350.

16. *Mandatory Vehicle Emission Inspection and Maintenance: Part B–Final Report, vol. V, pt. 2, Technical Analysis and Results*. Anaheim, California, Northrup Corporation and Olson Laboratories, Inc., 1971.

17. Orski, K.C. "Vehicle Free Zones in City Centers." Prepared for the Organization for Economic Cooperation and Development (OECD) Symposium in Techniques for Improving Urban Conditions by Restraints of Road Traffic, held in Cologne, October 25–29, 1971.

18. Private communication with Dr. Brian Ketchum, Director of the Office of Planning and Implementation, New York City Department of Air Resources, August 1973.

19. Private communication with David Kircher, U.S. Environmental Protection Agency Office of Air and Water Programs, June 1973.

20. Private communications from Lee Tinkham, Chief Engineer, Research and Development, Dynameter Division, Clayton Manufacturing Co., August 29, 1973 and February 1, 1974.

21. Rankin, W.W. "Report on Results from Right Turn on Red Light Questionnaire Survey." *Traffic Engineering* (1955) vol. 26, no. 1.

22. Remarks by James O. Boord, Assistant Director, Automotive Technical Service Department, Champion Spark Plug Company, March 1, 1973.

23. Schlaeffi, J.L.; Masher, D.P.; Ross, D.W.; Williams, J.O.; and Zeidler, H.M. "Chicago CBD Traffic Control System," vol. I. Menlo Park, California: Stanford Research Institute, Systems Analysis and Design, October 1971.

24. Smith, Wilbur. *Motor Trucking in the Metropolis*, 1969.

25. "A Study of Private Automobile Travel in Chicago's Central Business District." Chicago Area Transportation Study, Data Collection Division Technical Memorandum, February 8, 1972.

26. Weiss, Abraham. Special Report 120: "Labor Practices and Problems in Urban Goods Movement." In *Urban Commodity Flow*. Washington, D.C.: Highway Research Board, 1970.

27. Wendell, R.E.; Norco, J.E.; and Croke, K.G. "Evaluation of Pollution from Transportation Systems." *Journal of the Air Pollution Control Association* (February 1973) 23.

28. Zerbe, R.O. *The Costs of Inspection-Maintenance, Preliminary Report to the Argonne-Chicago Environmental Project.* Chicago: University of Chicago, 1973.

CHAPTER FOUR
MASS TRANSIT AS AN ENVIRONMENTAL TOOL

1. Basic Issues in Chicago Metropolitan Transportation. Evanston, Ill.: Transportation Center, Northwestern University, June 1958.

2. Bone, A.J. "Travel-Time and Gasoline Consumption Studies in Boston." Highway Research Board Proceedings, 1952.

3. Claffey, P.J. "Time and Fuel Consumption for Highway User Benefit Studies." *Highway Research Bulletin* (1960) no. 276. Cited in Johnson, M. Bruce. "On the Economics of Road Congestion." *Econometrica* (January-April 1964) XXXII:144.

4. "Crisis and Solution." Report of the Governor's Transportation Task Force, January 1973.

5. Duffy, M.K. "The Modal Split Policies: Costs and Benefits." Table 11. Unpublished paper, University of Chicago, 1973. Duffy's predictions are based on recent annual traffic count maps of the Illinois Department of Transportation. He assumes ADT grows at a rate of one percent a year.

6. Ergun, G. "Development of a Downtown Parking Model." *Highway Research Record* 369 (1971). 118–134.

7. Guttman, J. "Avoiding Specification Errors in Estimating the Value of Time." *University of Chicago Center for Urban Studies: Urban Economics Report No. 110,* 1973.

8. Haikslis, G. and Hyman, J. "Economic Evaluation of Traffic Networks." *Highway Research Board Bulletin* (1961) no. 306. Cited in Johnson, M. Bruce. "On the Economics of Road Congestion." *Econometrica* (January-April 1964) XXXII: 144.

9. Hay, G.; Morlok, E.; and Charnes, A. "Toward Optimal Planning of a Two-Mode Urban Transportation System: A Linear Programming Formulation." *Highway Research Record* 148: 20–38.

10. Hewitt, J. "The Calculation of Congestion Taxes on Roads." *Economica* (February 1964) XXXI: 79.

11. Hill, D.M. and von Cube, Hans G. "Development of a Model for Forecasting Travel Mode choice in Urban Areas." *Highway Research Record* (1963) 38.

12. Hurter, A.P., Jr. "Air Pollution, CBD Transportation and Mass Transit Costs." Report for Argonne National Laboratory, Center for Environmental Studies, September 1973.

13. Illinois Department of Highways, Traffic Surveillance Unit, Raw Data.

14. Keefer, L.E. "The Relation Between Speed and Volume on Urban Streets." Highway Research Board Report, 37th Annual Meeting, 1958.

15. Lave, C.A. "The Demand for Urban Mass Transit." *Review of Economics and Statistics* (August 1970) 52: 320.

16. Lisco, T.E. and Tahir, N. *Travel Mode Choice Impact of Potential Parking Taxes in Downtown Chicago Technical Paper No. 12.* Chicago: Illinois Department of Transportation, Office of Research and Development, 1973.

17. National Transportation Policy (Doyle Report) Preliminary Draft of a Report to the Senate Committee on Interstate and Foreign Commerce, 87th Congress, 1st Session. Washington, D.C.: U.S. Government Printing Office, 1961.

18. Morlok, E. et al. *Final Report: The Effect of Reduced Fare Plans for the Elderly on Transit System Routes.* Evanston, Illinois: Transportation Center Research Report, March 1971.

19. Rath, G. "Paying for Roads. The Economics of Traffic Congestion." *Second International Symposium on the Theory of Traffic Flow.* London: Office Environmental Control Development, 1963, p. 47.

20. R.H. Pratt Associates. *Low Cost Urban Transportation Alternatives: Vol. II. Results of Care Studies and Analysis of Busway Applications in the United States.* Washington, D.C.: U.S. Department of Transportation, Office of Urban Transportation Systems, January 1973.

21. "A Statistical Analysis of Speed-Results Hypotheses." *Highway Research Record* (1965) 154.

22. Vickrey, W. Cost Estimates Submitted to the Congressional Joint Committee on Washington Metropolitan Problems, 1959.

23. ——. "Some Implications of Marginal Cost Pricing for Public Utilities." *American Economic Review* (May 1955).

24. ——. *Urban Economics Report.* Chicago: University of Chicago, 1974.

25. Walters, A.A. "The Theory and Measurement of Private and Social Cost of Highway Congestion," *Ecoometrica* (October 1961) 29: 670–899.

26. Wagner, F.A. and May, A.D. "Volume and Speed Characteristics at Seven Study Locations." *Highway Research Bulletin* (1960) No. 281. Cited in *Highway Capacity Manual.* Washington, D.C.: Highway Research Board 1965, p. 46.

27. Wigner, Martha F. "Disaggregated Modal Choice Models of Downtown Trips in the Chicago Region." 446 *Highway Research Record,* 49–65, 1973.

CHAPTER FIVE
SUMMARY AND CONCLUSIONS

1. Zerbe, R.O. Optimal Environmental Jurisdictions, 5 Ecology Law Quarterly, 1 (Sept. 1974).

APPENDIX A
DAMAGES FROM
TRANSPORTATION POLLUTANTS

1. Babcock, L.R. "A combined Pollution Index for Measurement of Total Air Pollution," *Journal of Air Pollution Control* 20; 653 (Oct. 1970).
2. Babcock, L.R., Jr.; and Nagda, N.L. "Cost Effectiveness of Emission Control," 23 *Journal of Air Pollution Control* No. 3, Page 173 (March 1973).
3. Thomas, W.A.; Babcock, L.R., Jr., and Shults, W.D. *Oak Ridge Air Quality Index* (ORNL-NSF-EP-8), Oak Ridge National Laboratory, Oak Ridge, Tennessee, (Sept. 1971).

APPENDIX B
MASS TRANSIT COST MODEL

1. Hurter, A. "Benefit Table Report on Proposal to Use Gasious Fuels in Chicago Taxicab Fleet," Argonne National Laboratory: (Center for Environmental Studies, Argonne, Ill., August 1973).
2. Morlok, E.; Kulash, W.; and Vandersypen, H. *Final Report: The Effect of Reduced Fare Plans for the Elderly on Transit System Routes;* (Northwestern University Transportation Center Research Report, March 1971).

APPENDIX C
THE EFFECTS OF DEMAND ON
AIR QUALITY PREDICTION

1. Chow, G. "Statistical Demand Functions for Automobiles and Their Use for Forecasting" in A. Horberger (ed.) *The Demand for Durable Goods,* University of Chicago Press, 1960, 149–178.
2. Dyckman, T.R. "Aggregate Renewal Needed for Automobiles," 38 *Journal of Business,* 252–266, (July 1965).
3. Nerlove, M. "A note on Long Run Automobile Demand, 22 *Journal of Marketing,* 57–64, (July 1957).
4. Suits, D. "The Demand for New Automobiles in the United States 1929–1956" 22 *Review of Economics and Statistics* 60–75, (August 1958).

APPENDIX D
EMISSION PREDICTION AND
CONTROL STRATEGY

1. Bowditch, F.W. and Martens, S.W. General Motors Environmental Activities Staff, letters from July 6 and September 21, 1971.
2. Cernansky, N.P. and Goodman, K. "Estimating Motor Vehicle Emissions on

a Regional Basis." Annual Meeting of the Air Pollution Control
Association, June 14–17, 1970.

3. *Federal Register, Part II,* 36 (128): 12657 (July 2, 1971).
4. *Federal Register, Part II,* 36 (158): 15486 (Aug. 14, 1971).
5. General Motors. *Progress and Programs in Automotive Emissions Control.*
March 12, 1971.
6. McGraw, M.J. and Duprey, R.L. *Compilation of Air Pollutant Emission
Factors.* Preliminary Document. Washington, D.C.: U.S. Environmental Protection Agency, April 1971.
7. Ott, W.; Clarke, J.F.; and Ozolins, G. *Calculating Future Carbon Monoxide
Emissions and Concentrations from Urban Data.* Publication No.
999-AP-41. Washington, D.C.: National Air Pollution Control
Administration June 1967.
8. Pattison, J.N. "The New Federal Driving Cycle for Vehicle Emission Tests."
69th Annual Meeting of the Air Pollution Control Association,
June 27–July 2, 1971.
9. Research Triangle Institute. *State Motor Vehicle Inspection.* Durham, N.C.:
Environmental Protection Agency, July 1970.

APPENDIX E
RETROFIT OF IN-USE VEHICLES

This appendix was prepared with material obtained variously from:

1. Control Strategies for In-Use Vehicles, Washington, D.C.: U.S. Environmental
Protection Agency, November 1972.
2. Control Techniques for Carbon Monoxide, Nitrogen Oxide, and Hydrocarbon
Emissions from Mobile Sources (AP66), Washington, D.C.: U.S.
Department of Health, Education and Welfare 1970.
3. Conversations with engineers from General Motors, Ford, Universal Oil
Products, International Harvester and Gould.
4. Cumulative Regulatory Effects on the Cost of Automobile Transportation
(RECAT), Final Report, Office of Science and Technology, Washington, D.C. 1972.
5. Dewees, D.N., "Economic Analysis of Automobile Pollution Control Policies,"
Toronto: University of Toronto, January 1973.
6. Downing, P. and Stoddard, L., *Economics of Air Pollution Control for Used
Cars,* University of California, Riverside: 1973.
7. Horowitz, J., "Retrofit for Reducing Automobile Emissions: Effectiveness
and Cost," *Journal of the Air Pollution Control Association* 23,
May 1973, 395.
8. Report by the Committee on Motor Vehicle Emissions, Washington, D.C.:
National Academy of Sciences, February 12, 1973.

Index

air: cost benefit analysis, 103; downtown, 3; quality goals, 29
Atlantic Richfield Co., 46
automobile: age, 17; controls and new cars, 28; convenience, 73; maintaince, 98; mass transit, 76; parking, 100; pollutants, 1, 21, 98; retrofit,
Ayres, R.V., 38

carbon monoxide, 29; air quality, 7
catalytic converter, 94
CATS (Chicago Transportation Area Study), 20, 78
CBD (Central Business District), 5; parking ban, 58
Chicago, 3; bus lanes, 87; damage cost, 29; Department of Environmental Control, 47; emission decline, 30; LPG conversion, 59; mass transit, 72; Lung Association, 46; testing procedure, 44; Transit Authority map, 76
cities, 95; unique standards, 33; pollutants, 3
commerce: staggered hours, 66
congestion, 64, 71; hyper, 76; tolls, 81
control devices: costs, 23–25
cost: effectiveness, 9, 10; effectiveness of federal policy, 103;–of local controls, 42;–of local strategies, 66;–of retrofit, 33, 61; engine design, 38; estimation of car emission model, 22; fare policy, 85; highway use, 81; inspection maintenance, 47; mass transit subsidy, 91; nighttime delivery, 65; on-street parking ban; 58; pollution damage, 28; travel, 76
Creighton, R., 20

delivery, 58; off-hour, 63; reschedule, 97

emissions: Chicago, 30; control model cost, 23; effects, 59; federal program, 93; history, 11; local standards, 98; mileage, 17; reduction calculation, 45; reduction program, 8; standards, 2
EPA (Environmental Protection Agency), 2
Ergun, G., 79, 84

federal government: program evaluation, 38; test procedure, 12
fleets: cost-effective, 42; engine design, 37; vehicles, 17
freeways: bus lane, 86; Chicago, 3

gas: consumption, 37
Guttman, J., 79

Hay, G., et al., 9
health, 94
Hewitt, J., 80
Hurter, A.P., 75

inspection program, 41

Johnson, 79

Keefer, L.E., 78
Kitch. E.W., 60

land use, 20
lead, 29
LPG: conversion, 97; strategy, 62
Los Angeles: carbon monoxide, 1
Louisville, 87

mass transit: Chicago, 3; cost benefit analysis, 103; economies of scale, 87;

About the Authors

Richard O. Zerbe is currently Visiting Associate Professor of Economics at Northwestern University on leave from Roosevelt University, and also a member of a research team at the University of Chicago and Argonne National Laboratory investigating environmental problems. His writings in the environmental area have dealt with instruments for environmental control such as emission taxes and land use regulation, and with regulatory and jurisdictional aspects of environmental control. In the field of Economics his articles have concerned such diverse topics as antitrust law and economics and comparisons of theories of national income fluctuations.

Kevin Croke is presently on the faculty of the School of Public Health, University of Illinois Medical Center. He received his advanced degrees in Operations Research at Northwestern University and has specialized in the field of the economic evaluation of environmental protection programs. He has published widely in this field.